What people ar
Silence Your Inner Pharisee

Jon Fugler is real, he's human and he's a lot like you and me. That is, if you've ever wondered how to get free from trying to impress God. As Jon shares his story of struggle and search for intimacy with God, you won't learn "principles" for getting free. You'll actually *get* free. This book is your free pass to gaining the intimacy your heart has been longing for. Dive in!
>Todd Isberner
>*Men's mentor and author of* **What Every Man Needs to Know**

Passion vs. performance. It is easier to focus on the Kingdom work we do, rather than the passion for the lover of our souls. This quick read shows us how to focus more on growing our relationship with Christ than doing more to earn his favor. Such a good reminder, especially for those in full time ministry.
>Sandi Brown
>*Founder and President, JOY FM St. Louis*

I'm all about performance. I live, eat, and breathe it. Leading the effort for millions of people seeing the JESUS Film on TV every year, along with training and consulting globally, as well as working on a Master of Theology, I want to be a million-mina man! Then comes along Jon Fugler with his book, **Silence Your Inner Pharisee**, and he nails me right in the middle of my idolatry. Thanks, Jon. Thanks a lot.
>Tom Terry
>*Global Broadcast Strategy, Jesus Film Project*

Jon writes with "battle smoke" experiences.
>Lauren Libby
>*President, TWR*

I love this book! It's so needed by those of us who are driven to perform for God. We can get so busy serving Jesus that we have no room for *knowing* the Jesus we serve. Jon Fugler points us to a healthier relationship with Jesus based on love rather than performance. Knowing Christ intimately will change your life from *what* you do to *why* you do it.

>Wayne Pederson
>*Global Ambassador, FEBC*
>*Board Chair, The Joshua Fund*

I made my living for years by performing in front of tens of thousands of baseball fans. When I suddenly lost my ability to do that, my faith took a big hit. After several years of personal crisis and struggle, I found out what it really meant to know Jesus deeply. Jon's book, **Silence Your Inner Pharisee**, helps performers like you and me recapture the joy in our walks with Christ. I wish he had written this book 35 years ago.

>Dave Dravecky
>*Former Major League Baseball pitcher*
>*Author and motivational speaker*
>*Co-Founder, Endurance with Dave and Jan Dravecky*

I've known Jon for several years and have watched him live out what he writes in this book. You will see the love of Christ on each page as Jon calls us into a deeper walk with Jesus. My life has been enriched because of his understanding of what it means to say, "My relationship with God is the most important thing in my life."

>Dr. Peggy Banks
>*VP of Global Assistance*
>*International Christian Concern*

CS Lewis wrote, "If I find in myself desires which nothing in this world can satisfy, the only logical explanation is that I was made for another world." ***Silence Your Inner Pharisee*** escorts you to experience the One who built that 'other world' and thus the only One who can fully satiate your desires for the rest of your life.

> *Dr. Bruce McNicol, Co-Author*
> ***The Cure; The Ascent of a Leader; Bo's Cafe***
> *Founding Partner, President Emeritus,*
> *Trueface.org*

After years of performance Christianity, Jon learned the freedom of following Jesus. Truly, we do not *achieve* anything, but *receive* everything. Read Jon's words and reflect on his path to a breakthrough that could lead to yours.

> AJ Sherrill
> *Anglican priest and author of **Being With God: The Absurdity, Necessity, and Neurology of Contemplative Prayer***

Performance Christianity—a perfect topic for believers who are out there in hyper drive but losing the joy. We all can fall prey to the outward aspects of our "church" personalities without investing into the depth of relationship that our Savior desires. ***Silence Your Inner Pharisee*** is a profound work that will resonate with many.

> Rene Bravo, MD
> *Bravo Pediatrics*
> *Trustee, California Medical Association*

Also by the Author

Your Life With God: 30 Days of Joy

Your Life With God: 30 Fays of Faith

Your Life With God: 30 Days With Jesus

Your Life With God: 30 Days of Encouragement

Your Life With God: 30 Days of Incredible Prayer

Your Life With God: 30 Days of Courage

Your Life With God: 30 Days of Rest

Corona Season Continues: A Christian Response to the Pandemic

Silence Your Inner Pharisee

Ditch Performance and Embrace
Radical Freedom in Christ

Jon Edward Fugler

Fine Christian Books
North Carolina USA

©2023 by Jon Edward Fugler
Published by Fine Christian Books
North Carolina, USA.

All rights reserved. No portion of this book may be reproduced in any form without permission from the publisher or author, except as permitted by U.S. copyright law. For permissions contact: jon@yourlifewithgod.com.

First Printing, 2023
ISBN 9798390883167 (Paperback)

Cover design by Chris Lilly.

Scripture quotations marked (ESV) are taken from the ESV® Bible (The Holy Bible, English Standard Version®), copyright © 2001 by Crossway, a publishing ministry of Good News Publishers. Used by permission. All rights reserved.

Scripture quotations marked (NIV) are taken from the Holy Bible, New International Version®, NIV®. Copyright © 1973, 1978, 1984, 2011 by Biblica, Inc.™ Used by permission of Zondervan. All rights reserved worldwide. www.zondervan.com The "NIV" and "New International Version" are trademarks registered in the United States Patent and Trademark Office by Biblica, Inc.™

Scripture quotations marked (NASB) are taken from the (NASB®) New American Standard Bible®, Copyright © 1960, 1971, 1977, 1995, 2020 by The Lockman Foundation. Used by permission. All rights reserved. Lockman.org

To the Apostle Paul, whose life and words
have taught me what it means to know Christ.

Restore to me the joy of your salvation.

Psalm 51:12 (NIV)

Contents

1 From Bondage to Freedom 1
2 Knowing Jesus Brings Our Spirit to Life 9
3 Freedom From Performance 13
    Ralf's Story 21
4 Three Depths of Knowing Christ 23
    Lisa's Story 28
5 Hunger First 31
6 Thirsting for God 37
    Larry's Story 42
7 Knowing the Christ OF the Cross 45
8 Knowing Jesus and Being Conformed to his Image 51
9 Rise Above Circumstances 57
10 How to Know Jesus 61
    Noonie's story 72
11 The Diligence of Knowing Christ 75
12 How to Make Progress in Knowing Jesus 81
13 Trials Drive us to Know Jesus 87
    Parker's Story 92
14 The Presence of Jesus in Our Pain 95
    Jim's Story 100

15 Knowing Jesus as the Way, the Truth and the Life 103

16 Living Freely in Christ 113

    Tim's Story 118

17 Knowing Christ Consistently 121

Closing Thoughts on Our Stories 129

Acknowledgements 132

APPENDIX A: Exercises in Knowing Jesus 135

APPENDIX B: Retreating with Jesus 168

Other Books by Jon Edward Fugler 173

Go to www.freshfaith247.com/assessment

Foreword

There's a problem we face as followers of Christ. In the pursuit of godly Christian living, somehow the life can get sucked out of our most important relationship. The one with Jesus. And we don't even know how it happened. That's why it's a tremendous honor to write the foreword for Jon Edward Fugler's timely and transformative book, ***Silence Your Inner Pharisee: Ditch Performance and Embrace Radical Freedom in Christ***.

I've known Jon for several years and have worked with him in a variety of endeavors. Throughout our shared experiences, he has consistently demonstrated spiritual maturity, integrity, and the value of true friendship.

My journey in the music world began when I finished as a top six finalist on American Idol in 2007. This incredible experience opened doors for me to be signed as a recording artist and tour the world alongside some of the most prominent names in the music industry.

However, my performance ambitions and aspirations completely unraveled after leading worship at a youth conference in Asia. As I looked around the room and saw people responding to God's presence, I realized what an incredible platform I'd been given to share the gospel.

It was in this context that I first encountered Jon. At the time, he was serving with a global outreach ministry that aimed to produce a promotional single to raise awareness for their cause.

We immediately bonded over our shared passion for spreading the gospel of Christ to people worldwide. This connection set the stage for our ongoing commitment to making a difference in the world through the power of music and faith.

I've discovered that Jon is a man on a mission. Over the course of his impressive four-decade career in Christian media, he has served in a wide range of capacities, ultimately landing in his current role as chief content officer for TWR. This media ministry broadcasts in over 240 languages and reaches a staggering 190 countries and territories. He works tirelessly alongside his wife, Noonie, who collaborates on the development of global programming. This dedicated couple is committed to bringing the gospel to 4.2 billion people worldwide under TWR's signals.

Jon's personal story is one of remarkable transformation. His Christian journey began with a performance-based mentality, fueled by well-meaning advice to read the Bible for at least five minutes daily. This seemingly innocuous approach, and his background as an athlete, led him to relentlessly pursue spiritual success through an ever-growing series of checklists and how-to guides. While his dedication to his faith was admirable, it left little room for cultivating a deep, personal relationship with Jesus Christ.

In *Silence Your Inner Pharisee*, Jon shares his transformation from a life dominated by performance to one passionately focused on nurturing an authentic, personal relationship with Jesus. He leads us on our own personal journey to examine our approach to Christianity and pursue a more genuine, intimate bond with Jesus.

Jon's wholehearted endorsement of a life centered around Jesus, rather than the relentless pursuit of spiritual accolades, serves as a powerful and timely reminder of the true essence of Christianity. Through his own experiences, he demonstrates that authentic faith is not about ticking boxes or rigidly adhering to a set of guidelines. Rather, it's about developing a deep, intimate relationship with Christ that transcends performance metrics and expectations.

As you delve into the pages of *Silence Your Inner Pharisee*, prepare to be captivated by a compelling and heartfelt narrative that serves as a source of inspiration for your spiritual journey.

Jon will help you overcome obstacles and escape the grip of performing for Jesus. His insights will resonate deeply with those who have felt weighed down by the suffocating expectations of performance-based Christianity.

May **Silence Your Inner Pharisee** catalyze your spiritual journey, leading you to a life that is truly and unapologetically centered around Christ.

Sincerely,

Phil Stacey, *Christian musician and worship leader*
American Idol finalist
Author, **Made to Worship: Empty Idols and the Fullness of God**

Introduction

When it comes to the Christian life, there's a performer in all of us.

That's what a friend casually told me not too long ago.

His statement threw me. I thought I was a member of a small club of Christians locked into doing all the right things for Jesus. I pondered his words for several days. His statement may have been true, but he didn't understand one critical point.

For some of us, performance *dominates* our Christian lives. And it's slowly killing us. We tell ourselves we're right with God, but deep inside we know something is wrong.

That was my story for decades. And it may be your story right now.

Are we Pharisees? Oh no, not that!

Pharisees were some of the most learned, obedient religious leaders of the day. They knew the Law and they lived it out. But so many of them had equated their obedience to the Law with the health of their relationship with God. They looked shiny on the outside, but they were spiritually sick on the inside.

They were performers. And you might be one, too. You know the Bible, you've lived obediently, and yet you're unfulfilled.

You do the right things for God and even serve him well. But inside, something is missing.

I was there. For decades. And no one knew it except me.

I could recite the verse, "So if the Son sets you free, you will be free indeed" (John 8:36 NIV). And "It is for freedom that Christ has set us free" (Galatians 5:1 NIV). They were real in my head but not in my heart and life. I wasn't free. I was trapped.

Thankfully, I finally struck gold. I discovered a biblical truth that was right there in front of me during all those years of struggle. This truth, dramatically and clearly stated by Paul, has turned my relationship with Jesus into a consistently joyful experience. And it can for you. I feel like my newness in Christ has been returned to me.

You're in for an adventure as we unpack this life-giving truth in the pages ahead.

Let's ditch performance and embrace radical freedom in Christ.

You'll read my story and the stories of others who are on the path to freedom in their walk with Jesus.

This book is about changing your story. You can break free from the grip of performance Christianity.

You can silence your inner Pharisee.

1

From Bondage to Freedom

I grew up playing sports and loved it. I was the consummate competitor. Above all, I hated to lose. But sadly, winning and success were so expected of me, *by* me, that victory didn't bring joy.

My competitive flair shined brilliantly in non-stop matches with my best friend, Mertz. Baseball, hockey, ping pong. Batting and ball-throwing competition. Board games. Backyard battles. We even created games when we were out of games to play. Mertz and I competed with the best of them.

We had verbal competitions, too. I remember our constant debates over whether the American League or National League was the best. I was a die-hard NL guy and Mertz was AL to the core. We'd shout valid arguments across the street at each other, neither of us giving an inch.

Much of the time, our competitiveness went over the top. We would race home from school to go face-to-face at Mertz's ping-pong table in his family's beautifully-finished basement.

Would we play a game or two for fun? No. We would play World Series style, best-of-seven. But that wasn't enough. We'd play best-of-seven of best-of-seven. Two or three hours of intense competition, up to nearly 50 games! And we'd do it for several days in a row.

On the baseball diamond, I was a hard-throwing left-handed pitcher, living for the exhilarating challenge of blowing the ball by the hitter. Each batter was my enemy to conquer. I wanted to be perfect every time I walked to the mound. My standards were high. Too high. It led to discouragement and fits of anger when I didn't succeed. But that's another story.

My competitive lifestyle wasn't limited to sports. Whenever there was a chance to win at anything, I was ready to go. Board games, spelling bees, races to the bus stop, you name it. As my high school football coach once said, "If you're playing tiddlywinks, play with manhole covers." Maybe that saying contributed to my need to win ... every time.

> I accepted myself for what I did, not for who I was.

Performance was my friend. And my worst enemy. It became a demon that plagued me for decades, spilling unchecked into my spiritual life. I was conditioned to believe that my value was based on the way I performed.

I accepted myself for what I did, not for who I was.

When I gave my life to Christ as a 16-year-old, I remember the decision point. I thought to myself, "If God can accept me for who I am, I guess I can, too." That's when I went forward at a small country church on a cold, winter night, turning my life over to Jesus. By his grace, I was accepted for who I was and didn't have to live a performance-based life anymore.

But I still did.

My conversion had little effect on my attitude. In fact, I brought performance into my relationship with God. The drive to accomplish was so ingrained in my life that I couldn't escape its prison.

On that night of my salvation, I was told by a church leader that if I didn't do anything else, spend five minutes a day reading the Bible. That's the best advice in the world, because it fills our minds with the Word of God. However, that was one of the worst things you could have told me. It fed my performance-based mentality.

Like a good athlete, I read my spiritual training book (the Bible) faithfully almost every single day. For at least five minutes. I believe this routine kept me in the game with my newfound faith. I had no Christian friends and went to a dead church. The church where I came to Christ was 20 miles from home.

I knew nothing about growing in Christ. My Bible was my only hope. I was stranded with it for over a year, until a few Christians showed up in my life. But my spiritual input remained meager at best.

That was just the beginning. My next 45 years of my faith were characterized by what I call "performance Christianity."

I was taught how to have personal devotions or "quiet time." I made sure I did that faithfully so God would approve of me.

I was trained on how to share my faith. I learned that I must do that to live obediently for the Lord.

I led Bible studies because growing Christians do that. God would be happy with me.

I adopted James 1:22 as a life verse: "Be doers of the Word, not hearers only." How could a Bible verse like that be bad for me? It's a holy verse of Scripture, but it became the core of who I was. It took the place of Jesus at the center of my life.

I was eating up the how-to Christian life books that flooded the Christian marketplace in the '80s and '90s. Five steps for a thriving Christian marriage; seven ways to raise healthy children; the four pillars of Christian growth.

I went to many conferences where the Christian speakers affirmed the "step-by-step to spiritual success" philosophy of the books I had read.

Driven by performance for God, I thrust myself 100% into full-time Christian service right out of college. That environment fed my need to perform. Over the years, I became a Christian leader again and again in a variety of settings. It was the perfect world for me, but poised me for a disaster I never saw coming. The shell of Christian service was not supported by a core of a healthy relationship with Jesus. Too often, I was "playing" Christianity.

In my 30s, I imploded. Still, it took another two decades to discover freedom from the bondage of this works-based Christian life. I was locked into a pharisaical mindset.

I had mistaken performing for God for *knowing* Jesus. Wrapped up in activities and outcomes, I had consistently missed Jesus altogether. The lifestyle was addictive. The more I knew about "living" the Christian life, the more I wanted to know about it and how to do it.

I felt that I was growing spiritually. All outward signs were verifying that growth, while I was crumbling inside. I didn't know Jesus intimately. I knew *about* him and what I thought he wanted me to do.

> **Obedience to Christ and knowing Christ can be disguised by Satan as the same thing.**

Obedience to Christ and knowing Christ can be disguised by Satan as the same thing. The Father of lies, the devil, had me completely fooled. Absolutely, totally, 100% deceived. I had played right into his hands from the day I became a believer. I was fragile, missing what God really had in store for me. Relationship.

When God gave me the gift of my salvation, it wasn't his intention for me to slip into performing for him. I can imagine his tears as I repeatedly leaned into service rather than leaning into him.

Certainly, I had many, many spiritual victories and some incredible times of growth. I fell into the arms of Jesus in countless seasons over those decades. But the seasons were short-lived, fading away for years at a time. My default was performance Christianity, serving Jesus rather than knowing him.

In Ephesians 2:8, the Bible explains that we are saved by grace and that it is a gift of God. It has nothing to do with our efforts. However, once we are saved, too many of us fail to live by grace. We live by effort. Our society expects and rewards great efforts and achievements, and this is opposed to God's ways. No wonder it is a daily struggle to toss out our filthy rags of performance and humbly cling to Jesus as our only hope for spiritual health.

Isaiah 64:6 nails it: "All of us have become like one who is unclean, **and all our righteous acts are like filthy rags**; we all shrivel up like a leaf, and like the wind our sins sweep us away" (NIV).

Your problem of performing may not be as severe as mine, but this sin creeps into all our lives. We live in a world that honors, rewards and encourages performance. That's not a bad thing. In your job, you need to perform well. That's why you're there. As a parent, you should do your best. Student, you need to put forth effort to learn and get good grades. Husband, love your wife. Show it by actions.

Doing is good. But when we transfer that to our spiritual life, we can cave in if it takes over.

Here's something to consider. Instead of letting the world's ways spill into our relationship with God, what if we let our relationship with God spill into the world?

It's not a novel thought. Jesus said it this way, "You are the salt of the earth. You are the light of the world" (Matthew 5:13-14 NIV).

As Christians, we're supposed to love, serve, give, sacrifice, encourage and share the gospel.

But here's the problem. We're so focused on being salt and light that we've forgotten that the original Light, Jesus, is the light we are to shine. "In him was life, and that life was the light of all mankind. The light shines in the darkness, and the darkness has not overcome it" (John 1:4-5 NIV).

How can we shine the light of Christ unless we are closely knit to his heart? We can't. Our focus must be Jesus. Salt and light happen as a result.

You are in prison if you're living performance-based Christianity. You'll dry up, hate your life with God, seek worldly passions to satisfy, and end up broken and brokenhearted.

Are my words too strong? Take it from someone who has been there, those words are not too strong.

You might be there right now, or on the edge. You've been giving Jesus your best for years. You've faithfully obeyed and served him. You've led others to Christ or mentored them to maturity. You serve in the kids' ministry at church. You're in a Bible study. You lead a small group. You appear to be a stellar Christian example. You're doing all the right things.

Yet, you're dying inside. You know it but others don't. And you're ashamed to admit it because this shouldn't be happening.

Or, you could be on the opposite end of the spectrum. You've had it with Christianity. You're distant from God. He's a cold being rather than a warm friend. You've walked away from healthy spiritual habits. The Bible is dry, your prayers are empty, you're disillusioned with the Christian life and you have little or no desire to go to a church of any kind.

Friend, it's time for God to melt your heart. The better you *know* Jesus, the more your confused, hard heart will soften. Another way of putting it is that you'll be set free from the spiritual prison you've created for yourself. You thought it was a palace, but it has become a dungeon.

Jesus is waiting for you to meet him in a new way. On his beautiful, loving, grace-filled terms. He has no expectations more important than your relationship with him. This is where a vibrant spiritual life starts and continues. All the way to your last day on earth.

As I typed these words moments ago, it's remarkable that a friend texted me with this, "Dad took his last breath at 7:08 this morning. He is healed and is now with Jesus for eternity." Will your remaining time on earth be characterized by a life *with* Jesus, enjoying him *now* as you prepare for a life of eternity with him?

Jesus loves you. It's time to experience the world of relationship that you long for.

Your Story

I've told you my story. There's more to come. But what's *your* story? Throughout this book, you'll be able to work out your story and achieve true freedom in your walk with Christ. Some people are more trapped in performance Christianity than others. Let's discover where you are right now.

- In what ways can you relate to my story?

- In what ways can you *not* relate?

- How would you describe your Christian life when it was at its best? It may have been when you first came to know Jesus. Or it may have been when you had a spiritual breakthrough in your walk with Christ. Whenever it was, there was something special about that season. What words or phrases come to mind?

- I struggled with anger. Are there some issues or behaviors that you're struggling with? Take time to think about this question. Pray about it. Be open to what God may show you.

2

Knowing Jesus Brings Our Spirit to Life

Before we move forward, let's reflect.

"Very truly I tell you, no one can enter the kingdom of God unless they are born of water and the Spirit. Flesh gives birth to flesh, but the Spirit gives birth to spirit. You should not be surprised at my saying, 'You must be born again'" (John 3:5-7 NIV).

If your conversion was sudden, you can probably recall that day when Christ became your Savior. You were given new life. One moment you were spiritually dead and the next moment you were spiritually alive. Boom! You were born again. At that instant, you entered into an eternal relationship with Jesus. The Holy Spirit lit your dead spirit on fire and miraculously brought it to life.

Or maybe you grew up in a Christian home. Jesus has been part of your life as far back as you can remember. You went to church, youth group and summer camp. There's no date to pinpoint your conversion. However, there's likely a day you decided to do business with Jesus. Your parents' faith became your own faith. Do you remember that turning point? Whether that was your conversion moment, or it came earlier in life, you know you are born again.

The Holy Spirit came into you when you came to know Christ. As Jesus says in that passage, "The Spirit gives birth to spirit." Claim that truth as your very own.

This whole concept is quite mysterious. Yes, we are born again, spiritually alive, but it's hard for our minds to grasp the concept. Jesus affirmed that in the next verse. "The wind blows where it pleases. You hear its sound but you cannot tell where it comes from or where it is going. So it is with everyone born of the Spirit" (John 3:8 NIV).

You've got the Spirit, but you can't easily explain how He works. The more you know Jesus, the more clear this mystery will become.

Knowing Jesus is life-giving. His Spirit lives inside you. Your spirit has been brought to life, but that's just the beginning of your born-again experience. The deeper you engage with the Lord the more you'll experience his life. Like a baby that comes into the world, it's the start of something wonderful.

You might be reading this book because, as a born-again Christian, your spiritual life has taken a hit. No doubt, many hits. The spiritual adventure is not much of an adventure at all. What started as an exciting encounter with God has gone dormant, or at least it feels that way.

You aren't experiencing the new life Jesus gave to you on that day you were born again. You *have* new life, but it seems empty.

The wind isn't blowing. The mystery is gone.

"I should be more alive than ever," you say to yourself. "But I'm not. Where did that spiritual life go?"

The truth is, Satan is out to get you, to wipe out your faith. He wants to make you *feel* like a failure, *believe* that the Spirit of God doesn't live inside you and *deceive* you into thinking that you aren't born again. He wants to snuff out the fire. He can't do it, because Jesus ignited it. But Satan can sure make you *believe* you're spiritually dead.

If you're in that season now, the first thing you need to do is to claim your birthright. You're born again in the Spirit, Christ is your Savior, and that's that. Read the entire chapter of John 3 to see the full story of rebirth as Jesus explained it to a guy named Nicodemus.

Build on that truth. Knowing Jesus is a Holy Spirit thing. You can't do all the right things, follow the Christian rules or even be biblically obedient and expect your relationship with Christ to come alive. The Holy Spirit must be at the core of your walk with Jesus.

> The Holy Spirit must be at the core of your walk with Jesus.

It means that you need to get out of the center. You might not even know you're planted there. We live in a "get it done" society that has spilled over into our spiritual lives. I started my walk with Christ that way and lived it out faithfully for decades. I'm done with that. There's no going back. I am fed up with my performance-based Christianity. Are you fed up with yours?

When you hear someone say that you can achieve anything you put your mind to, reject that thought when it comes to your relationship with Christ. It is straight from the pit of hell. Satan wants you to keep struggling to achieve, to try to please Jesus and yourself. You'll fail.

There's a new way, which is really a very old way. It goes back to John 3. The day you first came to know Christ. The Holy Spirit brought you to life. Let him ignite the fire, just like he did on Day 1 of your spiritual rebirth.

Knowing Jesus is life. Knowing Jesus keeps the fire alive. Knowing Jesus puts him on the pedestal. It puts him at the center of your life. Yearn to know him above all other interests and activities. Let knowing Jesus consume you.

Your spiritual growth may have been stunted at some point. Through the power of the Holy Spirit, you can return to a vibrant life-giving experience of knowing Christ.

Your Story

Reflect on your conversion story. Write it out or make a few bullet points. It's good to reflect on your spiritual roots.

We can't experience the life-giving joy of intimately knowing Christ if we're at the center. It's a basic truth that you probably understand. But we can gradually slip into a lifestyle of self-effort instead of Christ-centeredness. If that describes you, will you take time right now and admit that sin? Then give the rightful owner, Jesus, his spot back at the center. When you do that, the Holy Spirit will work his transformation in your life.

3

Freedom From Performance

I've wrestled with the concept of knowing Jesus for quite some time. For how many years, I am not sure. But I do know that finally grasping this concept has rocked my world. I feel like I have come home. Knowing Jesus is the secret to life. Paul knew it. He stated it.

"What is more, I consider everything a loss because of the surpassing worth of knowing Christ Jesus my Lord, for whose sake I have lost all things. I consider them garbage, that I may gain Christ" (Phil 3:8 NIV).

There is richness and depth in that verse.

Knowing Jesus has freed me from the bondage of performance Christianity. Knowing him is like digging through several strata of rock and clay. Every strata is well-defined and we discover something new at every level. The Lord doesn't desire to be known at a distance. He desires close, deep, intimate fellowship with me.

We can know someone on the surface, but until we spend time with that person, we won't know them deeply. Time with Jesus opens the door for me to know him as he wants me to.

Let's go back to the rock and clay. We have to dig to get to the next layer and uncover its beauty and uniqueness. This takes time, effort, tenacity. So it is with my relationship with God.

I have to take time. Jesus doesn't get my leftovers. He gets my best time. My morning routine includes about a half-hour with him in prayer and the Word. Some days it's longer. Some days less. Honestly, I struggle with rushing. I find that my richest times of fellowship with the Lord is when I relax and enjoy him.

I have to be tenacious. Is every quiet time with Jesus filled with overflowing blessing? No. There are dry days when I'm tired, can't concentrate or preoccupied. That's life. That's the reality of relationship. But I come back the next day and seek his face. No matter how the time goes, I keep coming back. The life-giving experiences far outnumber the dry ones.

I have to put forth the effort. Hey Jon, you're getting into performance. No I'm not. Let me explain. Performance Christianity means that my relationship with Christ is defined by my effort. The more I put out, the closer I *perceive* I am to God.

On the other hand, putting forth the effort to know Christ simply creates an environment where I can develop intimacy with him. Also, as I put forth effort in prayer, listening to God, reading his Word and sitting before him, the richness of our relationship grows. My effort doesn't define the relationship. It makes relationship possible.

Time, tenacity and effort will lead to continued deepening of my relationship with Jesus.

Danger! Danger!

Let me wave a caution flag. As performers, we can be convinced that our efforts alone will open up the wonder of knowing Christ like never before. Oh, how easy it is to get into a controlling posture.

We can approach knowing Christ as if it's a hide-and-seek game. We think God is out there somewhere and we're doing our job to find him. He wants to make us work to get to know him. Our effort will determine his willingness to reveal himself to us.

The opposite is true.

In reality, God has the most important role in our relationship. He took the initiative to start it:

"For if while we were enemies we were reconciled to God by the death of his Son, much more, now that we are reconciled, shall we be saved by his life" (Romans 5:8 ESV).

We were enemies but he removed the barrier to knowing him. We didn't even know we needed to know Christ! Yet, Jesus died so we could taste a relationship with God. Why in the world would he give us a taste and then withhold the whole meal?

God is the one who opens our eyes, spirits and hearts -- or we'd never seek him in the first place. Look at these affirmations.

"No one can come to me unless the Father who sent me draws him" (John 6:44 ESV).

"All that the Father gives me will come to me, and whoever comes to me I will never cast out" (John 6:37 ESV). We can't resist God. Notice that God reaches out and we respond.

Our relationship with Christ is reciprocal. Jesus moves towards us *and* we move towards him. I love the way James puts it, "Draw near to God, and he will draw near to you" (James 4:8 ESV).

Psalm 145:19 assures us that "The Lord is near to all who call on him, to all who call on him in truth" (ESV).

Once we have a relationship with Christ, the Holy Spirit works miraculously to reveal more of Jesus to us. Without his work, we'd be stuck with our human ability to grow the relationship, never knowing Christ as God intended.

Our relationship with Jesus isn't a formula. It's dynamic, alive, ever-changing.

Our relationship with Jesus isn't a formula. It's dynamic, alive, ever-changing. We are both actively pursuing each other.

The biggest hindrance is us. God is present. His arms are open to receive us and know us. We need to continue seeking him.

The Bible is our #1 source on the life of our Savior. In order to know the Jesus that the Word describes, we have to stop and dig. Explore his character, study his actions and listen to his words recorded in Scripture.

Come back to my excavation with me. I'm carefully scraping the layers of rock and sand. Studying each piece and granule. Rubbing it between my fingers. Looking at it closely. Carefully. Curiously.

I think about the piece of stone in my hand. How old is it? How did it get here? What kind of rock is this?

Those are the kinds of questions I need to ask about my Savior and *to* him. I want to know as much as I can about him. His eternal history. His character qualities. Why he did what he did. Why he said what he said. Scene by scene. Layer by layer.

Can you imagine how the Holy Spirit will reveal more of Jesus than you've ever known? The possibilities are limitless. The more you know him the more you'll love him. And the more you love him the more you'll know him. It keeps getting better.

You'll walk in the most amazing freedom. The grip of performance will be broken.

That vibrant spiritual life you're seeking? You'll find it.

Paul is Our Model

If there was ever a hardcore servant of Christ, it was Paul. We read throughout Acts and his letters about his tireless service for his beloved Savior. While we tend to focus on that aspect of Paul, we often miss who drove him to such commitment to Jesus.

Paul spent his life knowing Jesus. He was wrapped up in it. I'm absolutely charged up when I consider his story.

His first *Jesus encounter* on the road to Damascus was too overwhelming to understand. He didn't know what hit him. Literally!

That was surface-level knowing. Jesus had so much more in store.

Paul spent the rest of his life, both in solitude and in intense firestorms, getting to know his Jesus. In all circumstances, his heart was set on knowing him.

Paul did some excavation, digging way below the surface to know Jesus more deeply. The more he dug, the more he learned new things about his Savior. For him, it was a treasure hunt. Knowing Jesus became a way of life for him. As a result, Jesus became his life.

"I want to know Christ—yes, to know the power of his resurrection and participation in his sufferings, becoming like him in his death" (Philippians 3:10 NIV).

We have to ask ourselves how deep we've dug to know Jesus. If we're not always digging, we're missing out.

Many loyal servants of God have fallen away from the faith. I believe a flawed relationship with the Lord led to their collapse. What appeared on the surface was not the reality below.

From his sufferings to his resurrection, Paul wanted to know the full scope of Jesus.

Knowing meant to immerse himself in the life of his Savior. Participation. Becoming like him through the power and working of the Holy Spirit (vs. performance).

Paul wasn't interested in being a bystander friend of Jesus. He wanted to be fully wound up in the life of Christ. Knowing him by experience.

- When Paul was shipwrecked, beaten, escaping death, he knew the Christ that was beside him in every instance.
- When Paul preached with power, often under distressing circumstances, he spoke with Jesus by his side. He spoke of a Jesus he knew personally and deeply.
- When Paul wrote his letters from prison, he sat there with his Savior, writing the words of God.

Everywhere Paul went, he had a conscious sense of Jesus' presence. He expressed it this way to believers in Rome:

"For I am convinced that neither death nor life, neither angels nor demons, neither the present nor the future, nor any powers, neither height nor depth, nor anything else in all creation, will be able to separate us from the love of God that is in Christ Jesus our Lord" (Romans 8:38-39 NIV).

Paul was confident to the core that Jesus was present with him. He knew the love of Jesus. Not as mental assertion, but by personal experience. In the barren prison cell, he felt the Savior's arms wrapped around him like a warm blanket. As a result, he gave praise to God even when shackled in cold, filthy irons.

No, nothing separated Paul from his loving Savior. And he understood it. No matter what the circumstance. None of the physical and spiritual warfare, nor any power, could come between Paul and Jesus' love.

You have a choice. Know Jesus or live without him.

Seriously.

If you're not connected closely to Christ, *experiencing* him, you're an isolated believer going through the motions of performance. That leads to emptiness.

Get to know Jesus. Dig, dig, dig. Know him in peace and know him in trials. Look to Jesus every minute of the day.

Above all, spend time in the Word. That's where you'll discover the wonderful layers of who Jesus is.

Will I someday know Jesus like Paul did? I hope so. In my optimism, I say yes. Truthfully, though, I don't want to go through the harrowing suffering that Paul endured. I'm soft. I hope I can know Jesus as intimately as Paul with a much less intense journey. Yet, in my heart of hearts, I know that's not possible. I'm still wrestling with this, as you might be.

I do know this: Whatever our lot in life, we are called to know Christ Jesus. Every one of our experiences will be different. We may know Christ in the quietness of our personal meeting space with him. Or it could be in our battle with cancer. Or loss of a spouse. Or enduring pain and illness. Or walking as the lone Christian at work. Or in the wonderful setting of a loving family.

Christ can be found and known anywhere. Today is your day to know Christ. Tomorrow is, too. And the next day. It's a journey. A journey that includes this moment.

Your Story

I have some *come to Jesus* questions for you as you work out your story.

- Will you set aside time to learn something about Jesus every day? Will you pray to your Savior each day? Will you put a circle of protection around your invaluable time with him?

If your answers to these questions are "Yes," then start today. If you already have a daily time with God, you're set up for exciting days ahead as you read further in this book.

Don't let others interrupt your time with God. Stow away, if necessary, even in a genuine prayer closet. Guard your fellowship with Jesus. You need it if you intend to know your Savior as he wants to be known.

Ralf's Story

From Duty to Delight

Twenty-five years ago, I read *Intimacy with the Almighty* by Chuck Swindoll. Going back further, in the early 1980s I read David Needham's book, *Birthright*. For the first time, I understood my identity in Christ and was delivered from legalism and performance-based Christianity.

Surely, I would never go back.

Yet, four years ago, as I assessed all aspects of my life, the picture wasn't good. How had I drifted so far back into a performance-based relationship with Jesus?

Here's how. I had become *driven* rather than *directed*. The spiritual disciplines—the means toward knowing God—had become a *duty* rather than a *delight*. Sadly they had deteriorated to a checklist instead of the path toward greater intimacy with Jesus. I had allowed what I was doing for God to become a substitute for my relationship with him. I was on the hamster wheel of performance Christianity and desperately wanted to get off.

Outwardly I looked like I had it all together, highly active in church through teaching, serving and leading. But inwardly, instead of resembling a healthy Psalm 23 sheep lying down in green pastures, I more closely resembled a stampeding bull.

I was Martha, banging pots in the kitchen and wrapped up in non-stop activity, instead of Mary who sat at the feet of Jesus.

I came across that familiar passage, "Come to me, all you who labor and are heavy laden, and I will give you rest. Take my yoke upon you and learn from me, for I am gentle and lowly in heart, and you will find rest for your souls. For my yoke is easy and my burden is light" (Matthew 11:28-30 ESV).

I prayed, "Lord please give me this rest!"

And he has. The past four years have been an amazing journey. This season of life has resulted in the richest time of growth in my 50+ year walk with the Lord. But it hasn't been easy. As a Type A personality, a hard charger, always ready to tackle the next task, there were changes I had to make.

First, I started with rest and life-balance. I began an in-depth Bible study on rest and the Sabbath. My reading list grew to over 35 books and other resources that spanned spiritual, mental, emotional, and physical well-being.

Second, I found a couple of like-minded Christian brothers to walk with, encouraging one another through the journey.

And third, I let go of unhealthy habits and began practicing healthy ones. I became unwavering in my pursuit of rest, making a commitment to eliminate anything from my life that even faintly resembled a performance-based—rather than a grace-filled—relationship with Jesus.

My journey continues but it's so worth it!

Ralf Stores is a pastor, media ministry leader and author of the blog The Rest Stop.

4

Three Depths of Knowing Christ

Knowing someone on earth is one thing, but *how* can we know the God in heaven?

Good question.

We can't reach out and touch Jesus. We can converse with him, but not in the way we would our spouse. I'm not one who audibly hears the voice of Jesus.

We can't go out to dinner together. Or ride bikes. Or spend a day at the beach with each other. Take a walk. Discuss the day when we get home from work.

In a sense, we can, but I think you know what I mean. Knowing Jesus is a whole different concept and needs a different approach than getting to know your spouse, kids or friends.

Let's go back to Philippians 3:8: "What is more, I consider everything a loss because of the surpassing worth of knowing Christ Jesus my Lord" (NIV).

I think there are three degrees, or depths, of knowing. They are progressive, but they overlap and continue our entire lives.

Intellectual Knowing

The first degree is *intellectual*. When I came to Christ, walking from the back of the church to the front, giving my life to him, my level of knowing was minimal. I didn't even know what I didn't know! That was the same for Paul at his conversion. Although he knew the Scriptures backwards and forwards, he didn't know Christ at all until his conversion. His intellectual knowing began.

As I look back, I realize that I knew only one thing about Jesus at the moment of my salvation: he loved and accepted me the way I was. Over the next year, God revealed more to me about the decision I had made that night. I learned about Jesus my Savior. I learned that he died for my sins.

I didn't learn much more. I was just trying to get my head around this new relationship. The learning curve was big.

I was growing in intellectual knowledge of Jesus.

Heart Knowing

The second degree is *heart* knowing. The more we know *about* Christ (intellectual), the more we fall in love with him. During that first year of my new relationship with Jesus, my heart began to soften. The relationship went deeper because my innermost being was connecting with my Savior. It was a process, but there was definitely a transformation from intellect to heart. As I considered that Jesus died for me, sparing me from hell, it moved me. That's when my journey with Christ really began to take shape.

There's an emotional element to heart knowing. When we know and connect with Christ with our heart, we're moved. The best place to better understand what it means to know God with our heart is in the book of Psalms. Notice the words David uses that indicate the intimacy of his heart relationship with his Father. This same intimacy is available to us with his son Jesus.

"*In peace* I will lie down and sleep, for you alone, Lord, make me dwell in safety" (Psalm 4:8 NIV).

"The Lord *has heard my cry for mercy*; the Lord accepts my prayer" (Psalm 6:9 NIV).

"The Lord is my shepherd, I lack nothing. He makes me lie down in green pastures, he leads me beside quiet waters, he *refreshes my soul*" (Psalm 23:1-3 NIV).

"The Lord is my *light and my salvation*—whom shall I fear? The Lord is the *stronghold of my life*—of whom shall I be afraid?" (Psalm 27:1 NIV).

"For great is your love, *reaching to the heavens*; your faithfulness *reaches to the skies*" (Psalm 57:10 NIV).

Open your Bible and a journal. Search the Psalms for more evidence of David's heart knowing of his Father. Write down the verses and underline the key heart knowing words. The Lord will show you what it means to know him with your heart.

Heart knowing is a lifelong process. We should grow deeper in love with Jesus throughout our life. Of course, there are interruptions, but a growing relationship with Christ is a deepening love relationship. The more we know Christ with our heart, the more we open up to him. That's a key part of heart knowing. Transparency with God.

In the process, he melts away our sin. Heart knowing deepens. When the Holy Spirit reveals our offenses towards God, our heart is grieved. This is a sign that our love relationship is growing. If our sin isn't melting away, our heart is probably hardened. I've gone through those seasons and so have you. But as we respond to God's softening, our heart knowing goes deeper and further. We fall more in love with Jesus.

There's a mystery to this process. God is the one who softens our heart, but we have to respond. That's what relationship is all about.

Experiential Knowing

I did a word study on *knowing*. I guess I wanted to know what it meant. It was fascinating. I learned that the word means to "experientially know." The third and most intimate degree of knowing Jesus is *experiencing* Jesus. Knowing Jesus like Paul knew Jesus isn't only about facts. It's about experience. Head vs. heart. Intellect vs. living.

The word study also revealed that it was a knowledge gleaned from first-hand (personal) experience. In other words, I can't truly know Jesus vicariously through my pastor. While I should be hearing solid, inspiring, biblical sermons about Jesus, that doesn't replace my responsibility of knowing him *first-hand*.

Experiencing Jesus is when we integrate mind, heart and life. Knowing Christ when hard times hit is *experience*. Knowing him when we're broken in our sin is *experience*. Knowing Jesus when loss crushes us is *experience*.

Experiencing Jesus happens in some of the darkest and most challenging times of our lives. My wife's battle with cancer turned into a season of knowing Jesus. We came to the throne of grace over and over again, standing in the presence of our Lord. Personally, I spent many stretches of time pouring my heart out to Jesus, in tears at times. Then I soaked in his love, peace, care and strength. Cancer season brought me closer to Jesus. I felt I knew him well in this season of suffering.

Paul knew Christ experientially. In his shipwrecks, beatings and persecution, you bet he knew Christ. That's because he knew Christ intellectually and with his heart. He was prepared for experience. For life. A tough life. That's why he was able to say, "I have learned to be content whatever the circumstances" (Philippians 4:11 NIV).

On the other end of the spectrum, knowing Jesus doesn't have to come in trial. He wants to know us daily, to enjoy him. Any close friendship goes through the highs and lows of life experiences, but the relationship exists mostly in the normal in-between seasons. You do life together, enjoying each other. When we choose to turn to Christ in daily life we are *experiencing* him.

Jesus desires that we come to know him in all seasons, not only when we face the hard times. We need our Savior every day.

Experience begins with time spent together. Earlier, I said that knowing Jesus is nothing like knowing a friend or spouse. At the core, however, it is. Many of the same principles and practices apply. Spending time together with Christ lays the foundation for knowing him in the battles of life.

So how do we go past the intellectual and into the *experience* of knowing Jesus? It makes sense to study Paul for some clues. After all, he said his life goal was to know Jesus.

But before we do, we need to have a heart-check. Is your hunger to know Christ really there?

Your Story

This is not a black-and-white question. But respond with the first answer that comes to mind. It's likely the truth.

- How *deep* do you know Christ these days? Is it centered mostly around intellectual knowing, heart knowing, and/or experiential knowing?

Today, tell Jesus you want to get to know him *fully*—intellectually, heart knowing and experientially.

Then, as you spend time with him and in his Word, be sensitive to how he reveals himself to you in your mind and heart. Be prepared, too, for opportunities he brings your way to know him experientially.

This is an important piece of your story. Don't rush through it. In your time with Jesus every day, come back with the same request to know him *fully*. Your relationship with Christ will become richer. You'll recapture the joy that's been missing.

Lisa's Story

Communing with God Through Prayer

Abiding in God is my life passion, and prayer is at the very heart of this intimacy. Communing with God takes on many forms throughout my day.

When I awaken, I align myself with the Father and his purposes. Daily, I ask, "Father, what are your plans for me today?" It is a laying down of all of *my* plans, agenda and expectations. I invite God to help me see him, myself, others and my circumstances through his eyes and with his love.

Settling into the Lord's Prayer, I expand each section. As I pray, I surrender anew to his kingship and will, embrace my dependence on him, confess my sin and appeal for his deliverance from evil and temptation.

Then, putting on the armor of God, I remind myself of what is true. I am "in Christ" and everything I need for life and godliness has been given to me to live victoriously for him today. This is not just a daily pep talk; it is a declaration of Scriptural truth that is foundational for my day.

At other times, I commune with God through musical worship and walks in nature. As my soul worships him in song, I intersperse prayers of thanksgiving and praise. On our walks together in creation, I look for the characteristics of God that are demonstrated through what he has made. He may show me his *creativity* in the variety of tree bark textures I notice or the many songs of the mockingbird. His *provision* is revealed so beautifully after a rain shower when drooping flowers open and stand tall.

I also love to commune with God while studying the Bible, looking up the meaning of words and digging into the cultural context. It requires taking time to slowly read and hold this Word of God, reflecting on it, listening and receiving it into my life. He may lead me to ponder a single verse and to ask the Spirit to give me his insight. Reflecting and journaling during these times has become a way of capturing what God has shared and to record my thoughts and responses.

Yet, my most essential time to commune with God is when I simply come to him to know him better – to listen to his heart. He has impressed on me so often, "Do not come to me for what I can do for you. Come near to know me, to seek my heart. I will guide you in the areas that you need my help, but it will be in my way and in my timing. Just seek me."

I have to adjust my entire life to make this happen. For only when I radically slow down do I have time to listen to him. It involves quieting my soul in his presence and waiting on him.

Communing with God through prayer has profoundly changed my life. It has deepened both my love for God and others as I choose to live in him.

Lisa Hall has a passion for prayer and serves with TWR Women of Hope.

5

Hunger First

I've been a writer as long as I can remember. It started when I "published" a neighborhood newspaper. In reality, it was one typewritten page of stories like "Man Bites Dog." I thought the idea was phenomenal, but since this was before copy machines, PCs and printers, typing each paper individually shut down my newspaper business after that first issue.

However, my creative juices have flowed ever since then. As a middle school student, a few friends and I formed a baseball league using a board and spinner game called All Star Baseball. We kept statistics, standings, followed a schedule and, yes, published a newsletter. By then, I had access to my school's ditto machine and was able run off 50 copies at a time—with permission, of course!

My budding publishing career went dormant for a few decades, primarily because I was occupied with real life. It wasn't until I was in my 40s that another venture blossomed. I became the publisher of several regional editions of the *Christian Times* newspaper. This lasted for 10 years, until newspapers faded into the sunset. I loved the creative thrill of publishing and distributing a new issue each month to many California cities.

Then came the adventure of writing books. I took a stab at self-publishing a sports book related to a business I owned. I learned the ropes of publishing Kindle, print and audio book formats. The thrill of the book arriving, hot off the press, is something that still causes my heart to jump. The book continues to sell, much to my delight.

What I've learned over the years is that I'm a content creator. In the midst of my book-writing venture, I became conflicted. The concept of knowing Jesus started to rise to the surface. What God was showing me went against what I had learned and practiced since I was 16.

There are three books in my life that have changed my trajectory. One of them transformed my thinking about how to live the Christian life. It's called *With: Reimagining the Way You Relate to God*, by Skye Jethani. My friend, Jeff, handed me the book and said it had changed his life. It did the same for me, so I went on to buy several copies and gave them away.

The bottom line in the book is this: We fall into one or more traps in the way we primarily relate to God. These traps kill our spiritual vibrancy, health and freshness. They actually distance us from Jesus instead of drawing us to him. Jethani makes the strong point that God wants us to enjoy a relationship *with* him.[1]

A relationship *with* God. This simple concept really shook me up. The light went on. I realized I had lived my Christian life as a faith-*performer* for God. I wanted this new life *with* him. It immediately shifted my thinking.

I read the book several times. I couldn't get this simple, yet deep, principle out of my mind.

Jeff and I talked about it. I discussed it with my wife, co-workers and other friends. I read the book again, highlighting this time. I tried to wrap my head around this new way of thinking. It was hard. I had to unlearn the wrong ways I'd related to God, then learn the right way. After decades of learned behavior, I found it nearly impossible. I kept falling back into my old ways.

---

[1] The other two books that have changed my life are *Radical* by David Platt and *Being With God* by A.J. Sherrill. I highly recommend them.

In the past, I'd feel guilty. I knew I wasn't living for God like I thought he wanted me to. Frustration came and went. I kept *doing* for God and wasn't satisfied. Christ still seemed distant. I was lonely, even though people were around me. I couldn't express the tension inside me. Often, I'd get angry, certainly a poor expression of a vital relationship with Jesus.

Imposter syndrome, otherwise known as hypocrisy, would weigh me down. After decades of being a Christian, why wasn't I feeling and living a vibrant life with Jesus?

But that was the past. Now I began to respond in a healthy way. This is when I began to silence my inner Pharisee. Knowing what I learned from Jethani about a relationship with God started to trickle into my life.

Thankfully, I made progress over the long-term. Two steps forward. One step back. I started climbing out of my performance hole.

Journaling helped. A third time through *With* also made a difference. But my approach to my time with the Lord was the biggest factor that changed my life.

God gave me a simple set of statements that I call my Statement of Faith. It's not about what I believe, but it's about who I want to become as a Christian.

For an entire year, I focused on the first statement:

My relationship with God is
the most important thing in my life.

I still feel a sense of relief when I read and say that sentence. It's like taking a deep breath and exhaling. It has revolutionized my relationship with God.

Focusing first on that relationship, everything else then comes into perspective. All of life cascades from a right relationship with God. That relationship has to be my #1 focus. I had it backwards for 40 years. I was doing things for Jesus and equating it to the health of our relationship.

The Lord gave me two Bible verses to anchor my statement. The first was, "Love the LORD your God with all your heart and with all your soul and with all your strength" (Deuteronomy 6:5 NIV). That's what life is all about. Loving God. With my heart. With my soul. With my strength. Not with my performance. My service for God is an outgrowth of my love relationship with him.

I spent weeks considering what it meant to love God. It was an adventure. God and I grew in intimacy.

Couple that verse with this next one and it epitomizes a fully committed, loving relationship. "For God so loved the world that he gave his one and only Son" (John 3:16 NIV). The Father gave his only son because he loved me so much. Jesus died for me because he overflowed with love for me. Praise the Lord that he took the initiative to move towards me when he went to the cross. I picture God reaching out to me from heaven, and he does. He welcomes me with loving, open arms.

Jesus is all-in with me. And I'm all-in with him.

This new version of my relationship with God breathed life into me. I was like a kid. The newness of my relationship with Jesus came back. Now, every time I read my statement, it's fresh.

My relationship with God is the most important thing in my life.

Relationship is a two-way street. God gives all of himself to me and I give all of myself to God (not *for* God). That is one tight relationship.

I had a breakthrough. For an entire year, I kept coming back to that statement. I haven't shared it with many people (until now!) because it was personal. Between God and me. I felt a sense of sacredness in the statement and held it close to my heart. Perhaps I wanted to test and experience it for a while to see if it played out in my life.

It has.

That was seven years ago.

By making the statement that "My relationship with God is the most important thing in my life," I was able to intentionally trust Jesus with the rest of my life. I still had responsibilities coming out of my ears, but I shoved them aside in my mind every morning when I came back to my sacred statement. I was *enjoying* God. I felt relief, freedom, joy.

In fact, over a year later, I wrote a 30-day devotional called *Your Life With God: 30 Days of Joy*. I poured out on paper what God was doing in my heart, hoping I could be a blessing to others. This led to several other devotionals on faith, courage, rest, encouragement and prayer. They all center on Jesus and our relationship with him.

I'm anti-performance, and these devotionals take the reader to the heart of God, to the feet of Jesus.

I can honestly say that I hunger for Jesus, wanting to know him as Paul did.

I want you to hunger for Jesus. If you're anything like me, you'll find that it's a long process. But every single step has been an incredible joy. It's been fun. An adventure. I'm communing with God like never before. I have a long way to go to know Jesus like Paul did, but the journey is fulfilling and life-changing.

I learn new things every year. The Lord introduces me to people who help me go deeper. Like A.J. Sherrill, Bruce McNicol and Bryan Russell. These people experience Christ to a degree I can only hope to. The point is, we have to be hungry learners.

I invite you to come along. If you're hungry, satisfy the hunger by knowing Jesus. Know the Christ of the cross, the one who has been here since all eternity and who will be here for all eternity. There's so much of him to know.

My hunger, my quest, is like Paul's: "I want to know Christ—yes, to know the power of his resurrection and participation in his sufferings, becoming like him in his death" (Phil 3:8 NIV).

Next, let's explore *thirsting* for God.

Your Story

Most of the time, the reason we don't hunger for God is that we're satisfying ourselves with other things. Unsuccessfully. We lose our desire to know Christ. We drift into living *for* God instead of living *with* him.

- Now is a good time to pause. Go to the Lord in prayer. Ask him to give you a deep hunger for him. Also, be honest and ask him to reveal those satisfaction substitutes that are in your life. We all have them. Is there a sin that has a hold of you?
- Confess these things to God. Thank Jesus that he died to release you from bondage and gives you freedom in your relationship with him.

Make a *habit* of asking God to give you a hunger for him.

And, if God lays a statement of faith on your heart, write it down. It was a big part of my life-change.

6

Thirsting for God

"I thirst for you, my whole being longs for you" (Psalm 63:1 NIV).

Knowing Jesus isn't an activity. It is a state of being. In this Psalm, David's physical setting reminds him of his spiritual setting. He's in the desert of Judah, "a dry and parched land where there is no water" (verse 1b).

He looks around him. Desolation. He looks inside. Desolation. In thirsty desperation, he says that his whole being longs for God.

Have you ever gone so long without water that your mind and body deteriorate? The further you drift into that state, the more helpless you feel. And when you realize you don't have a water source nearby, panic starts to set in.

I used to live in Colorado Springs, well over a mile-high elevation. The altitude and dryness sucked the water right out of my body. Guzzling bottles of water was necessary for survival.

If I went without my H2O, it would take just minutes for the effects to set in. First, my mental sharpness and concentration would dissipate. Then I'd feel achy. Before I knew it, I was becoming dehydrated. My attitude would change, too. I'd be cranky. All because I wasn't hydrated.

Finally, when I'd remember to grab a drink of water, I'd gulp down two or three glasses out of the tap (the water in Colorado is delicious). Slowly, my senses would return. My mind and body would come back to normal.

God gave us physical thirst to remind us how much we need him.

Just as we can't merely take a sip of water in the desert, we can't take a sip of Jesus on occasion. We need to satisfy our thirst for Jesus always.

I'm reminded of the Samaritan woman whom Jesus met at the well in John 4. She was thirsty, so all she had on her mind was water.

> "Now Jesus learned that the Pharisees had heard that he was gaining and baptizing more disciples than John—although in fact it was not Jesus who baptized, but his disciples. So he left Judea and went back once more to Galilee.
>
> "Now he had to go through Samaria. So he came to a town in Samaria called Sychar, near the plot of ground Jacob had given to his son Joseph. Jacob's well was there, and Jesus, tired as he was from the journey, sat down by the well. It was about noon.
>
> "When a Samaritan woman came to draw water, Jesus said to her, "Will you give me a drink?" (His disciples had gone into the town to buy food.)
>
> "The Samaritan woman said to him, "You are a Jew and I am a Samaritan woman. How can you ask me for a drink?" (For Jews do not associate with Samaritans.)
>
> "Jesus answered her, 'If you knew the gift of God and who it is that asks you for a drink, you would have asked him and he would have given you living water.'
>
> "'Sir,' the woman said, 'you have nothing to draw

with and the well is deep. Where can you get this living water? Are you greater than our father Jacob, who gave us the well and drank from it himself, as did also his sons and his livestock?'" (John 4:1-12 NIV).

Jesus turned the conversation in a different direction, using her physical thirst as the touch point to speak of her spiritual thirst. He said he was the Living Water and that we will never thirst when we experience him.

"Jesus answered, 'Everyone who drinks this water will be thirsty again, but whoever drinks the water I give them will never thirst. Indeed, the water I give them will become in them a spring of water welling up to eternal life.'
"The woman said to him, 'Sir, give me this water so that I won't get thirsty and have to keep coming here to draw water'" (John 4:13-15 NIV).

We must constantly come to the well. Come to Jesus, your Living Water.

The more you do, the more you will know him. Spending time with Jesus is the best way to experience and know him.

Yet, we often do this out of duty. We're supposed to meet with God for "devotions," aren't we? That word in itself turns me off. It goes against *relationship* and speaks of *duty*. Our motivation for meeting with Jesus must come from a genuine thirst for him.

Do you thirst for God, as David's whole being did?

If not, could something be wrong?

I contend that you do thirst, but you don't always realize it's for God. David knew that his God was the only remedy for his parched soul.

However, we try other things to satisfy the thirst only God can satisfy. We miss Jesus altogether. Our time with him becomes a burden. We leave unfulfilled, thirsty still. So we turn to work, our kids, hobbies, entertainment and social media to meet the need.

But these things are sips of water that never reach our souls.

Oh, please change your attitude about meeting with Jesus. He's such a patient God, showing up every day in your life. He waits for you to show up because you love him. How sad it would be if your kids spent time with you as a duty. Your heart would be wounded. You're there for them because you love them, and you desire the same from them.

You thirst. You thirst for God. You thirst for God with a longing soul. Those are facts. Wonderful facts. Recognize why you're thirsting and dive into a precious, loving encounter with Jesus. Today. Tomorrow. The next day.

No matter how tempting it can be, don't fill your emptiness with a Jesus substitute. Fill it with him.

Your Story

Read Psalm 63:1-8. Think about each verse. Picture David speaking to God. Imagine him being in the desert of Judah as a visual reminder of his thirsty soul. Put yourself in his sandals. And cry out to God with your longing, thirsty soul.

> "You, God, are my God,
> earnestly I seek you;
> I thirst for you,
> my whole being longs for you,
> in a dry and parched land
> where there is no water.
>
> I have seen you in the sanctuary
> and beheld your power and your glory.
>
> Because your love is better than life,
> my lips will glorify you.
>
> I will praise you as long as I live,
> and in your name I will lift up my hands.
>
> I will be fully satisfied as with the richest of foods;
> with singing lips my mouth will praise you.
>
> On my bed I remember you;
> I think of you through the watches of the night.
>
> Because you are my help,
> I sing in the shadow of your wings.
>
> I cling to you;
> your right hand upholds me" (NIV).

Larry's Story

Breaking Free From Performance and Rules

On the California Central Coast, we have some warm, sunny days in January. The morning on this day was chilly, but the forecast called for more comfortable temperatures as midday approached. I could sense Jesus inviting me to the beach, but I was hesitant to take the time off work. I often feel like I'm not "doing enough," a lingering failing tied to my performance mindset.

That's when I heard the still, small voice of the Holy Spirit saying, in effect, "Yes, that's the point. Your heart needs to be refilled. Will you join me?"

Thankfully, I made the right decision and decided to walk along one of my favorite stretches of the coast. When I arrived, not many people were there. I was able to simply stand at a scenic cliff and absorb the beauty of the view, breathing in the fresh smell of the ocean. To my surprise, tears began to fall quickly. "Be still my son."

While I stood on the cliff, absorbing the view, Jesus began to comfort me. He slowly revealed the anxiety I'd been feeling for the past month about planning my wedding. My engagement over Christmas was perfect. But being someone who likes to schedule things well in advance, Jesus was asking me to relax and trust him with all the details.

The sound of the waves crashing against the rocks below, the sun reflecting off the water, the smell of the ocean breeze and the beautiful scenery brought a keen sense of God's presence. As I wiped the tears from my eyes, I simply nodded my head up and down in a "yes" gesture. Then I said the words out loud, "Yes, Jesus, I give you control." What a relief to give him my anxiety of trying to control the upcoming wedding plans!

The next two hours were filled with prayers of thanksgiving to God for being so faithful to his Word in Joel 2:25, "I will restore to you the years that the swarming locust has eaten" (ESV). How refreshing to my soul as I let him speak to me through the beauty of his creation. He was reminding me of how he had brought so much healing and comfort to my heart after a crushing betrayal six years earlier.

Driving back home from the beach and listening to Christian music on the radio, a song played with the words that spoke of peace, joy and love on a new horizon. I found myself laughing out loud, singing the lyrics at full volume, while picturing Jesus in the passenger seat next to me singing, too. It was a wonderful way to conclude my extended time of prayer with my very personal Savior!

Performance almost stole a special day.

Thank you Jesus, for bringing me a new horizon of hope by being in your presence.

Larry Walters has served in media ministry throughout the years and loves to disciple men.

7

Knowing the Christ OF the Cross

When I tell friends I want to help people know the Christ of the cross, they picture Jesus hanging there *on* the cross. Indeed, the cross is central to coming to know Jesus, but it is not the whole story of who he is. Jesus is eternal. I want to know him in all his everlasting existence.

What do I mean by that?

John says, "In the beginning was the Word, and the Word was with God, and the Word was God. He was with God in the beginning. Through him all things were made; without him nothing was made that has been made. In him was life, and that life was the light of all mankind" (John1:3-5 NIV).

Jesus is the Word and was there in the beginning. John clarifies it in verse 14: "The Word became flesh and made his dwelling among us. We have seen his glory, the glory of the one and only Son, who came from the Father, full of grace and truth."

Look at all the rich words that describe Christ.

- The Word
- All things were made through him (Ultimate Creator!)
- Life
- Light
- Dwelled among us
- Glory
- Grace
- Truth

We could spend years diving into the depths of these qualities of Jesus. Imagine getting to know his glory. His truth. His grace. There's no finish line to knowing Christ. We go deeper, discovering afresh the amazing Jesus that we have come to know.

Jesus hung on the cross. We should never lose sight of that. Thanks to his sacrifice, we have the privilege of knowing him and his Father. Without the cross, there would be no relationship at all. With the cross, we have a starting point in our relationship, which will extend into all eternity.

> **With the cross, we have a starting point in our relationship, which will extend into all eternity.**

However, we worship not just the Christ *on* the cross, but the Christ *of* the cross. The Christ *on* the cross is a snapshot. The Christ *of* the cross is Jesus of eternity. He is both the Savior Lamb and the Lord of all. So we need to know all of him to worship him fully.

We dig and dig. We learn and learn. We know and know. There's no finish line. It's not a race. It's a digging to the depths. Every layer contains something new about Jesus. It's a marvelous lifelong journey.

I'm so excited about this that my keystrokes are punching out the wrong letters. I'm making corrections as I go. The thought of knowing as much of Christ's fullness and eternal being as I possibly can is phenomenal. There's power, fulfillment and joy in this lifelong experience. It won't end on earth. We get to continue the journey even more fully in heaven. I'm supercharged!

Who is this Jesus of the cross? Why did he die for us? Why does he want to know me and for me to know him? What was he thinking on that day he created man? These are just a few questions that come to my mind.

Then I dash forward to John's words in Revelation, describing the Christ of the cross. Here are some highlights from Revelation 1:12-18. I've taken the liberty to make a list so the impact is clear.

"I turned around to see the voice that was speaking to me. And when I turned I saw seven golden lampstands, and among the lampstands was [...]

- Someone like a son of man.
- Dressed in a robe reaching down to his feet and with a golden sash around his chest.
- The hair on his head was white like wool, as white as snow.
- His eyes were like blazing fire.
- His feet were like bronze glowing in a furnace.
- His voice was like the sound of rushing waters.
- Coming out of his mouth was a sharp, double-edged sword.
- His face was like the sun shining in all its brilliance.

"When I saw him, I fell at his feet as though dead. Then he placed his right hand on me and said: 'Do not be afraid. I am the First and the Last. I am the Living One; I was dead, and now look, I am alive for ever and ever!'" (NIV).

This is a far cry from the Jesus we picture *on* the cross. Look at the vivid words John uses to describe our beloved Savior in all his power and glory. Don't you get chills when you read these extraordinary verses? This is what I mean when I say that I want to know the Jesus *of* the cross. I want to know all of him for all time. The cross is the dividing point between death and life, Jesus moving from the weak man we observe, in overwhelming pain, to the Almighty God John portrays here.

Jesus' declaration to John is a mighty climax. Look again: "I am the First and the Last. I am the Living One; I was dead, and now look, I am alive for ever and ever!"

Oh, I want to know Jesus and as much of his fulness as possible – from the beginning of creation, through Revelation and all the way through eternity. Remember Paul's words in Philippians 3:10? "I want to know Christ—yes, to know the power of his resurrection and participation in his sufferings." He wanted to know all of Jesus. And at the time, he didn't know the fulness of Jesus described in John's Revelation. God had amazing things in store for Paul once he met his Savior face to face.

To know Christ in his eternity is to know him in his magnificent breadth and depth. From the eternal beginning to the eternal end of time. And every minute in between. This is the most thrilling adventure of your life. You have an awesome privilege to enter daily into a personal, lasting, loving relationship with the God of the universe, Jesus of eternity.

Let's spend our lives knowing the eternal Jesus, the Christ *of* the cross.

Your Story

- How does the concept of knowing the Christ *of* the cross differ from knowing the Christ *on* the cross?

For some reason, we have a hard time seeing all of Jesus' extensive character and attributes. It's as if he is a diamond and we only see a few facets. For me, I have an easy time seeing and trusting in Jesus' power and greatness. I think that's why I have a big faith. But I miss out on seeing his love and care.

- How about you? Which qualities of Jesus are easiest for you to see and experience? Which are the most difficult? Spend some time thinking about these questions and then note your answers. You'll see some gaps. You have an adventure ahead as you get to know more of who Jesus is.

In Appendix A, I've included 10 devotional experiences that will help you dig deeper into some of the many identities of Jesus. Spending time in these will reveal more of Jesus to you, helping you move into knowing him more fully. We need to move closer and closer to knowing the full, eternal Jesus.

8

Knowing Jesus and Being Conformed to His Image

Sheltering at home during the Coronavirus pandemic caused some strained relationships to completely break down. Irritations became unbearable. People we thought we loved (family) were almost unlovable after a month locked up together.

On the other hand, there are other people we would long to be quarantined with. (We'd probably get annoyed by them, too). I'm speaking about those few people we deeply admire. They have the qualities we desire. We look up to them. We listen when they talk, sharing gems of wisdom. We might even study their lives.

One of those men in my life was Sid. I had been a Christian less than two years when he took me under his wing to lead me further into spiritual maturity. I admired Sid. In fact, I spent so much time with him for a year that I started to behave like him. He was my role model and did a good job of it. Sid built healthy habits into my life that are still present today. He modeled Christ. I noticed and followed.

Who is your Sid? It might be someone who took time with you. Or is taking time today. It may be an author you read, a speaker you watch or listen to, a podcaster you take in. These days, your greatest influencer doesn't need to be someone you know. We have access to role models in many forms and on many platforms. You begin talking like them, thinking like them, even acting like them.

Hang around them long enough and you'll be a clone.

How would you like to be like Jesus? Not WWJD (What Would Jesus Do?) but HWJB (How Would Jesus Be?).

You will be. It's your destiny.

One of my favorite verses in Scripture is a promise in Romans 8:29: "For those God foreknew he also predestined to be conformed to the image of his Son" (NIV).

That means I'm going to be like Jesus someday! When I get to heaven, my sin will be banished and I will be like my Savior. Worry-free. Sinless. Joyful. Forgiving. Loving. Humble. Compassionate.

Think about it. You're going to be like Jesus.

A life-long earthly struggle will be eliminated. Have you ever wanted to be perfect? You will be when you come into Jesus' presence after your time on earth.

Billy Graham put it this way:

> "Think of it: Not only will all wrongdoing be banished, but everything that happens now because of sin's grip on this world will be gone forever. Illness and death will be destroyed; sorrow and disappointment will be no more; the faults in our characters will be transformed.
>
> "Think about those elusive qualities that keep reminding us how human we are. They're tucked away in Galatians: love, joy, peace, patience, kindness, goodness, faithfulness, gentleness and self-control. We want them but they're so elusive. When we're like Christ, every one of these qualities will be ours. Jesus personified."[2]

---

[2] (https://billygraham.org/answer/we-will-be-perfect-and-without-sin-in-heaven/)

As we explored earlier, spiritual rebirth happened when you came to know Christ. His Spirit gave you new life. The gift of his Holy Spirit is the secret to transformation into Christ-likeness. That happens the more fully we know our Savior.

Do you want an honest assessment of how well you know Christ? The depth of knowing Christ can be measured by the evidence of Christ in your life—the fruit of the Spirit that Billy Graham referred to. It's an outward indication of an inward working. It comes back to that most important relationship in your life—the one with God.

Ask your spouse or close friend to tell you how consistently you're showing the fruit of the Spirit. That's the most candid assessment. Don't ask for performance sake, but for *knowing* Christ sake.

Most Christians want an easy road to the fruit. We're told that we simply have to yield to Jesus, be filled with the Spirit and the fruit will show. As a result, we'll be a patient, loving, faithful, joyful Christian.

It's deeper than that. You need to immerse yourself into your relationship with Jesus. Fruit isn't the objective. Knowing Christ is. The more you know Christ, the more you'll be conformed to his image (Romans 8:29), thus bearing fruit more consistently. The Holy Spirit works in and through you as you draw near to Jesus in an intimate relationship.

> The more you know Christ, the more you'll be conformed to his image.

You'll constantly face the tension to drift into performance Christianity, trying to bear fruit in your own power. Certainly, you want to have love, joy, peace, patience, gentleness and all the rest. But the secret is to get your eyes off the fruit and on Jesus.

To have your eyes on Jesus means you have to know him. And to know him comes back to spending time with him. Quarantine yourself with Jesus. Often. I guarantee you'll know him. And become more like him.

Being conformed to the image of Christ doesn't only happen by spending time with him. It's in real life that his character emerges.

But it's rooted in your relationship with Jesus.

Mark's Stellar Example

My good friend Mark is a joyful believer. He loves Jesus. He's one of the guys I want to be like. I see Christ in him all the time. I think he has a corner on the fruit of the Spirit, because he's full of love, joy, peace, patience, kindness – need I go on? You get it.

What you don't know about Mark is his bout with non-Hodgkin *and* Hodgkin lymphoma nearly 20 years ago. Or the stem-cell transplant that saved his life. Or the years of nerve pain he has endured from the damage from the chemo treatments. He has had two surgeries to insert a neuro-stimulator to ease the pain. He lives with regular two-hour nights of sleep. And if that's not enough, he recently had two heart attacks, followed by inserting a pacemaker and defibrillator.

You're in pain reading this, aren't you?

Despite two decades of hardship that has almost cost him his life multiple times, Mark displays the fruit of the Spirit to everyone. In pain, he still smiles. When he is wiped out, his conversations are miraculously energetic. When financial hardship overwhelms him, he keeps trusting God. Mark always wants to know how I'm doing, rather than focusing on how he is feeling. He keeps giving glory to Jesus. On top of that, he is active in pursuing his passion to take Christ to those who have never heard the name of Jesus. He still serves in ministry several hours a day.

You might wonder how he does it. It's simple. Mark knows Jesus. He spends hours and hours in prayer. While he has a passion for the lost, his greatest passion is knowing Christ. And that comes from spending time with him. He prays alone and he is also part of prayer movements around the world.

Mark is being conformed to Christ because he has chosen to know him. When hardship comes, the depth of his relationship with Jesus shines through.

You might be going through trials right now that are wearing away your freshness with God. I encourage you to spend *more* time with Jesus. That's where the fruit is formed. That's where you become more like him.

While we will become fully conformed to the image of Christ when we meet him face-to-face, every day of our lives is an opportunity to get closer to that perfect image.

One of God's greatest treasures awaiting you is to be conformed to the image of his Son. It's a gift! Nothing you can earn. As you were saved by grace, you are conformed by grace.

Knowing Jesus is at the heart of this.

Your Story

- As you consider the fruit of the Spirit, which qualities are most evident in your life? Write them down in one column. Which are least evident? Write those down in another column. Be daring and ask your spouse or a close friend what they think.

As you know Christ more fully, the fruit of the Spirit will become more evident. In a few months, come back to this page and answer the questions again. See if God is changing your life. This is how you'll really see how well you *know* Christ.

It's healthy to come back to key Scripture passages in your journey to knowing Christ. Commit Romans 8:29 to memory: "For those God foreknew he also predestined to be conformed to the image of his Son" (NIV).

9

Rise Above Circumstances: Know the Power of His Resurrection

There are many benefits of knowing Christ. One of them is knowing the power of his resurrection.

Paul was yearning for it. "I want to know Christ—yes, to know the power of his resurrection" (Philippians 3:10 NIV).

What does it mean to know the power of the resurrection?

The New Living Translation puts in this way: "Experience the mighty power that raised him from the dead."

Knowing the power of the resurrection is experiencing the power that raised Jesus from the dead.

It's easy to view this power as physical or spiritual strength. If so, we've missed the most important effect of the resurrection: freedom from the penalty of sin, thus eternal life! When Jesus rose from the dead, he proved he was God, crushing Satan for good. The power of the resurrection is the key to our justification and regeneration. Our salvation is tied to it.

Paul experienced the power of the resurrection, just as you and I do now. But it's such a deep concept. The more we think about it, the more mind-boggling it is. You can spend the rest of your life marveling over this truth.

You've been raised from the death sentence of sin, given new life in the Spirit and will be raised from the grave as Christ was, into the full presence of God's glory. Multiply that by the billions of people throughout history who know Christ and that, my friend, is power!

The more you know Christ and the power of his resurrection, the more you'll affirm Paul's statement, "Since, then, you have been raised with Christ, set your hearts on things above, where Christ is, seated at the right hand of God" (Colossians 3:1 NIV).

As your mind is set on things above, you'll experience the joy of eternal hope. You'll rise above circumstances, knowing that your God is over all, greater than anything thrown at you in this world. Whether it's a terrible health ordeal, blown-up marriage or financial disaster, you'll look to the risen Jesus. He is there to carry you through.

> Whether it's a terrible health ordeal, blown-up marriage or financial disaster, you'll look to the risen Jesus.

The person who *knows* Jesus will turn to him. However, if we're not already engaged in our relationship with Jesus, experiencing him daily, we won't likely turn to him. We'll turn inward instead of upward.

Practice turning to Christ in the small challenges. Exercise your relationship with Jesus. You'll be encouraged as you see him work in your life. Your faith will grow. Your courage will be strengthened. Peace will flow. Joy will return. You'll build a habit of trusting him.

Paul beautifully explains the dynamics of our relationship with Jesus. "Continue to work out your salvation with fear and trembling, for it is God who works in you to will and to act in order to fulfill his good purpose" (Philippians 2:12-13 NIV). It's a together thing. We move towards God and, at the same time, he moves towards us to do his work in us.

The power of the resurrection is the apex of God's might. This infinite power crushed Satan, vaporized the penalty of sin, delivers hope daily to all believers and will, in the end, transport us from earth to heaven.

The power of the resurrection defeats the power of stress. *Look to the risen Jesus.*

The power of the resurrection overcomes the sorrow of losing a loved one. *Look to the risen Jesus.*

The power of the resurrection rules over the fear of cancer. *Look to the risen Jesus.*

The power of the resurrection conquers the bondage of performance Christianity. *Look to the risen Jesus.*

This is freedom. And it is exactly what we receive when we experience the power of the resurrection. It is freedom from sin and freedom to live in the power of the Holy Spirit.

You can rise above circumstances with the power of Christ's resurrection. You can experience this power, just as Paul did. Indeed, he knew the fellowship of Christ's sufferings when he was beaten, battered and bruised throughout his missionary career. But, oh, how he knew the power of the resurrection and the power of the Holy Spirit. His confident hope of eternal life with his Savior helped keep him steadfast.

He set his heart on things above. As a result, he was able to say, "I have learned the secret of being content in any and every situation, whether well fed or hungry, whether living in plenty or in want" (Philippians 4:12 NIV).

I believe his secret was tied to his lifelong goal to know (experience) the power of the resurrection. And that came from knowing (experiencing) Christ.

That's our mandate today.

Your Story

The resurrection of Jesus Christ was the ultimate demonstration of God's power. First and foremost, it put us in right standing with God. The penalty of sin was wiped out for all who repent and receive the gift of eternal life only found in Christ.

"For the wages of sin is death, but the gift of God is eternal life in Christ Jesus our Lord" (Romans 6:23 NIV).

- Where do you need to experience the power of the resurrection in your life today? With a relationship challenge? In your finances? Marriage? Parenting? Health? Work issue?

- Write down the details and begin trusting God for these things. In the days ahead, record how God shows up for you, especially how he changes your heart towards him.

10

How to Know Jesus

This could be the most important chapter in the book.

When I tell Christian friends that I want to help 1 million *believers* know the Christ of the cross, they're not impressed. I'm not trying to shock them with the number, but with the concept. *Knowing Christ.* I'm all worked up about it and they have glazed looks in their eyes.

Their face is saying, "That's nice." They're probably thinking, "Every Christian knows Christ, don't they?"

By now, you understand what I explain to them. Knowing Christ isn't a one-and-done deal. I unpack it this way:

*"You came to 'know' Christ when you came to faith in him. But it was just the beginning. You know your best friend so much better now than when you first met. You've done life together for years. You've shared your hearts, lifted each other up, held each other accountable, laughed together, cried together, counseled each other and you've bonded in a special way. Knowing Christ is the starting point in your journey. And knowing Christ **is** the journey."*

Try that with your Christian friends and you'll have a lively discussion.

Knowing Christ was Paul's lifelong purpose. It didn't have an end. He pursued Jesus and knowing him all his life.

How?

So if we are to know Christ better (and more intimately) as each day or week passes, the next question is, "How?" It's nice to have that lofty "Paul" goal of knowing Christ and the power of his resurrection, but how do we see it happen practically?

First things first. Let's understand that God has the major part in this. The spotlight shines on the Trinity. Jesus has a distinct role. So does the Father. And the Holy Spirit could be the most important person in the mix.

Knowing Christ, just like living out our walk with God, is not about self-effort. It's about faith and grace. Christ living his life in and through us. When we have the attitude that we should work as hard as we can to know Christ, we've missed the point. It's not a *doing* thing. It's a *being* thing.

> It's not a *doing* thing. It's a *being* thing.

Certainly there are actions to take, but don't get wrapped up in the actions. If you do, you'll miss Jesus altogether. You'll check off the actions, mistaking them for knowing Christ.

Knowing Christ has a facet which has nothing to do with us. It's true that hardship, tragedy or trial will cause our faith to reach a depth not possible in any other way. This proving ground almost always hits us from the outside. Our heart is pained, so we cling to Jesus. We pray. We search the Word for help and encouragement. We ask other believers to pray for us. We seek their counsel. Our eyes point away from the world and towards God.

For some believers, hardship seems always present.

A friend of mine has lived in constant discord for as long as I've known him. After years of moving up the ladder in his career, he lost his job. He and his wife lived in the desert for many months. He took a low-level position in a totally unrelated field just to put food on the table. Still, they lost their home and moved in with his wife's parents. It was humbling.

Once God provided a job in his field again, health issues hit. He was laid up for days at a time. He had serious surgeries to try to solve severe and lingering problems. To this day, he still lives in pain.

Meanwhile, their grown kids have had tragic difficulties. This has included substance abuse, marriage failures and attempts at suicide. While my friend and his wife were reeling from their own earthquake, they stepped in to help calm the storms in their children's lives.

It was a low season. Although he is now gainfully employed, there are still aftershocks from their kids' problems. The drama continues, but things are improving.

Through it all, my friend and his wife have faithfully trusted God. Their secret? They know Christ. I've seen it. It's the only way they can endure such hardship. Not only endure, but stay active in ministry in their church, family and workplace. Like Paul, they relentlessly know Christ.

I think of brothers and sisters in Third World countries. They struggle to put food on the table. They are surrounded by disease. Some are persecuted for their faith. Life is hard. Yet, they are often the most joyful Christians anywhere. They have nothing. But they have everything—Jesus. They have learned to *know* him and the power of the resurrection and the fellowship of his suffering.

However, none of us wants to constantly go from trial to trial to know Jesus better.

Most of life happens *between* the trials. How can you hunger to know Jesus as deeply *as if* you were in the middle of hardship? That's the challenge.

A Pure Heart

It starts with a pure heart. And that begins with coming to Jesus. When you're battling through a trial, you're probably honest with Jesus. You don't hide anything. You're desperate. You pour out your heart.

In the normal flow of life, that same transparency is needed if you're to know Christ deeply.

> **A good introspection leads to a good cleansing.**

A good introspection leads to a good cleansing. Not that we should get into a confession frenzy, but we are sinful people. Sin dwells in our heart.

Check your thoughts and attitudes as you come before Jesus. Think about the words you've spoken to others in the past few days. How have you behaved? In the presence of Jesus, run these things through your mind. Expose them to the Lord. Admit your sin and affirm his cleansing through confession. "If we confess our sins, he is faithful and just and will forgive us our sins and purify us from all unrighteousness" (I John 1:9 NIV).

What a magnificent promise!

Then repent, turning away from the sin you've confessed. Repentance isn't a simple action. We're pulled in by sin, so we have to intentionally turn away from it. A full 180 degrees in the opposite direction. Your heart needs to do an about face.

If you are serious about knowing Jesus, you need to be the real you. No hiding from the Lord. Part of knowing Jesus will be the eradication of sin in your life, as much as it is possible on this side of heaven. Paul struggled with sin and so will you. He said, "I do not understand what I do. For what I want to do I do not do, but what I hate I do" (Romans 7:15 NIV).

His solution? The truth of this statement: "Therefore, there is now no condemnation for those who are in Christ Jesus, because through Christ Jesus the law of the Spirit who gives life has set you free from the law of sin and death" (Romans 8:1-3 NIV).

Paul knew Jesus was the one who gave life and freedom. Our Lord removed any condemnation of sin.

Can you see why it's so important to come to Jesus to confess your sin and recognize the cleansing and freedom he offers? This will ignite fire in your relationship. Your openness will create a transparency that leads to closeness with God.

You'll be on your way to knowing him at a new depth.

This isn't a once and for all experience. Keep coming to Jesus. When sin creeps in, don't be afraid to confess it to him. He's waiting with open arms. He wants a rich relationship with you even *more* than you want with him.

God may reveal sin in your relationships with others. How can you come before the Lord with a pure heart when you have an offense against another person? You can't. You'll have to go to them and clear the slate by asking forgiveness. This is all part of removing those barriers between you and God.

Receive His Love

Doesn't it bring joy to your heart when your children know you love them? They come running to you when you walk in the door. They crawl up on your lap or, if they're too big for your lap, they give you a big hug. When they need help, they come freely to you. You joke around, play games, laugh together, cry together. All because they feel safe and free in your love.

We often have a hard time receiving the love of Jesus. We hardly consider it. This can be a major roadblock to knowing Christ. We're left with knowing *about* Christ, but not knowing him like Paul.

I often spend a half day with God. No agenda. Just a time to connect on a deeper level, uninterrupted by anything. I shield myself from my phone, isolating me from the outside world. Prayer, journaling, Bible study and sometimes Christian music are part of my experience. It's so refreshing and purifying.

One of those times, I decided to take Jesus with me and show him around. We went bike riding, hiking, spent time talking at a local fast-food restaurant and enjoyed a couple other activities. Why did I do such a crazy thing? I wanted to have time with Jesus in my ordinary world. I know he's interested in the details of my life, just like I'm interested in the details of my kids' lives. It's fun when they take me into their world and we do things together. So I did the same with Jesus.

I was walking with a friend the other day. He told me about a wonderful habit he and his wife have. They invite their grandchildren for an overnight a couple times a month. I'm envious, because our closest grandchildren are 500 miles away.

During the sleepover, my friends' grandkids are loved on with chocolate chip cookies, a kids movie and a variety of unplanned activities. I'm sure they learn about Jesus, too, during bedtime stories or dinner conversations.

These little ones are growing closer to their grandparents as every year goes by. They're getting to know them in the context of life. Phone calls and video chats are nice, but that doesn't cut it when it comes to knowing their grandkids. My friends are pouring out their love on the kids and the kids are receiving it. Fast forward 10 years and imagine the bond of love and knowing that will exist.

Do you receive Jesus' love? Or is your relationship *defined* by prayer and Bible study? While these habits are vital in knowing Christ, there's so much more potential in your relationship with him. To make it full and complete, there needs to be informal time with your Savior.

For instance, my half days with God are on my calendar, but there are no rules.

My friends' overnights with their grandkids are scheduled, but how they spend the time together varies.

We need a balance between structure and freedom in our relationship with Christ. Our love relationship will grow in those freedom times.

In structured and unstructured times, spend some of it reflecting on Christ's love for you. John 3:16 can become academic rather than overwhelmingly moving. Jesus loves you so much he gave his very life that you might have yours. Meditating on that verse and truth can make your head and heart spin. It's a staggering thought.

There are so many other truths about Jesus' love for you that are worth hours of consideration in an unrushed environment. Search the Scripture for them. Then camp on one truth for 15-20 minutes, letting your mind run wild as you think deeply about it.

How deep is Jesus' love for you? So deep that he has made it possible for you to join his family. "See what kind of love the Father has given to us, that we should be called children of God; and so we are" (I John 3:1 ESV).

A long time ago, a friend encouraged my wife and me to "waste time with our kids." That's great advice.

Waste time with Jesus. Your relationship with him isn't an obligation. Don't define the time by the clock. Take a deep breath. Loosen up. Enjoy Jesus and receive his love. It's essential if you really want to know him.

Love Him

There's a heart-wrenching passage in John 21. With all the disciples looking on, Jesus has a one-on-one conversation with Peter. It's all about love.
"Simon son of John, do you love me more than these?" he asks in verse 15.
"Yes, Lord," he said, "you know that I love you." Peter wouldn't have answered otherwise, would he? He was an all-in, 100% vocal follower of Christ.
Jesus continued questioning. So he asked his disciple the same question. Peter responded affirmatively, but he may have been less confident, sensing Jesus was probing below the surface.
Jesus asked at third time, "Simon son of John, do you love me?" (verse 17).
This time, Peter grieved. Perhaps his Lord didn't believe him or Peter realized he didn't love Jesus the way he had twice stated. Peter answered with more emphasis, "Lord, you know all things; you know that I love you" (verse 17).
Peter came to terms with his love for Jesus. And at such a crucial time. Jesus would soon leave the disciples, and he was choosing Peter to lead the young Church, or as Jesus put it during that love conversation, "Feed my sheep" (verse 17). Jesus wanted to make sure Peter's heart was right, that at the core he truly loved the Savior. That was a prerequisite for his service. It was a "come to Jesus" moment indeed.
I don't think it was a done deal at that moment. I imagine Peter spent the next several days wrestling with the genuineness of his love for his Lord. This watershed conversation would play in his mind long after Jesus ascended into heaven.
How's your love for Jesus?
Peter was ready to wholeheartedly serve his Savior. Certainly,

Jesus wanted him to feed the sheep, but first he wanted Peter's love. Not his allegiance. Not his service. Not his enthusiasm. Not his sacrifice. Not his grand works. But his love. His heart. That was most important to Jesus.

Isn't that incredible? With the future of Christianity at stake and a world to reach, above all of that the Savior of the world wanted a rich, love relationship with Peter. And he wants the same with you.

Are you loving Jesus merely by the things you do for him? Or are you loving Jesus by first investing time to be with him and know him?

Bible study is great. So is serving at church. Obeying the Word of God is essential. Giving generously to the Lord's work is living out your faith. Feeding sheep by discipling or mentoring other believers is right in line with God's will.

However, don't get caught up in the Peter trap. Although your works can be evidence of your love, they are not the core of your love relationship with Jesus.

> Although your works can be evidence of your love, they are not the core of your love relationship with Jesus.

With this treasured relationship at the center, a whole new adventure with Jesus opens up. Your service for him takes on a fresh meaning. Your faith walk comes alive. Giving, serving and feeding are inspired by your love for Jesus and empowered by his Holy Spirit.

Because you love Jesus, you'll discover that your actions for him will deepen your love further. It's a wonderful cycle.

If you feed sheep without loving Jesus, it becomes a hollow ritual that you'll abandon before long. Love Jesus and feed sheep.

Love Jesus and you'll know him more deeply.

Live Joyfully with Him

As I passed by the coffee station at my ministry office, I heard two co-workers laughing. Suddenly, I stopped, looked at them and announced, "Stop laughing! This is a Christian organization." Then I walked on, with a sly grin.

As Christians, we often take our relationship with Jesus too seriously. We need to laugh with him. I'm sure the disciples and Jesus had a few outbursts together. And imagine all those times when the men didn't get his parables. Our Savior probably chuckled when he explained the truth from three different angles.

"OK guys, you look confused. Let me unpack it a different way. There was this farmer..."

When I was in grade school, lunch was my favorite class. I'd join all my friends as we shared our lives and sandwiches. Lots of stories, laughs, boasting and ... noise!

Until the principal walked in. Talking stopped. Laughing subsided. A hush fell over the entire room as he slowly walked past each table. If any of us had done something wrong that morning, we were sure we'd be pulled out and escorted to his office.

To this day, I don't know why silence reigned whenever he entered, but it always did. I guess we felt we were supposed to act that way. Some sort of military inspection by the General.

Too often, we view Jesus as our principal. Silence is demanded. Laughing isn't allowed in his presence. Be quiet and eat. I'm sure my principal didn't want us to think or act that way, just as Jesus doesn't today.

We can be too stilted in our relationship with Jesus. We live out the Lordship part, honoring Jesus as Master. However, some people have a hard time living out the love part. Once you understand how much Jesus loves you, your heart will be flooded with joy. You'll be like a kid with your hero – excited, laughing, talking, having fun together. Every moment with Jesus will become a rich experience.

Are you living joyfully with Jesus? If not, you're missing out on a valuable dimension of your relationship with him. He's your friend. Like any other friendship, fun and happiness should abound. In prayer, share things that make you smile. Bounce ideas off of him. Be informal in your conversation. Let your guard down when you talk with him. Be the real you.

You can't really know him until you loosen up and enjoy him. Live joyfully with Jesus.

Next?

The title of this chapter is *How to Know Jesus*. You might think we didn't deal with that. But we really did. What we've covered here lays the foundation for what's next.

Your Story

Knowing Jesus as a way of life, as deeply *as if* you were in the middle of hardship, is a challenge.

- A pure heart is necessary for an intimate relationship with Jesus. Sin is a barrier. Take some time now to quietly examine your heart before the Lord. Ask him if there's anything between you and him or between you and another person. If there is, confess your sin to God and thank him for his forgiveness.

With a pure heart, you'll receive Jesus' love more fully than ever. You'll love him more intimately. You'll live more joyfully.

Noonie's story

The Invitation

The date printed on the new green journal is January 1. The first entry reads, *"Thank you Lord for the start of a New Year. Only You know what is ahead. Your perspective is perfect and full. I trust You with my life, my family, my friends, and all that matters to me. I love you. Help me to worship you into this year with my very life. Psalm 89:15 'Blessed are those who learn to acclaim You.'"*

Thirty days later, I was talking with a friend on my cell phone on a cold Colorado winter afternoon. Gazing out the window, I was holding the phone with my right hand. My left hand was seeking warmth under my arm when I halted the conversation. "Wait…wait…wait!" I said to myself. "Why am I feeling a Cadbury egg under my arm?"

My mind raced to the calendar. Jon and I were leaving in the morning for a 10-day ministry trip to Australia. I knew I had a routine mammogram scheduled for the day after we returned. So off we went to the land down under. As much as I tried not to think about it, my mind fixated on the fact that my medical future might be about to change.

A few days after my mammogram, my doctor scheduled a biopsy. The days crawled by as my husband and I waited for the results. Finally, we were asked to return to meet with the radiologist. We waited quietly, pensively, in the lobby for my name to be called. When it was, we were escorted into the only room that was unoccupied—a nearby supply closet.

The doctor's words were, "The biopsy is not good. There is cancer found in the tumor under your arm, but we couldn't find the original tumor in the breast." As he continued talking, Jon couldn't get around the word "cancer." He tuned out and pretty much began a journey of trauma.

As I heard the word "cancer," a visual of a small *white board* immediately came to mind, with my name on it. Next, the words, *Noonie's Agenda*, were being erased and replaced with *God's*

Agenda. In that moment, I experienced a peace, knowing that God was in charge of this breast cancer journey and I was on a ride-along. It was as though a thick fleece blanket was placed around my shoulders, assuring me that I'd be cared for and protected through all that was ahead.

At the time, I was reading the *Jesus Calling* devotional by Sarah Young. She reminded me that God was with me, watching over me. He is Immanuel (God with us), his presence covering me in his radiant love. I read that nothing can separate me from God. And that God has given me a gift that I am not to reject.

My 18-month breast cancer journey turned out to be an *invitation,* not a diagnosis. An invitation to one of the most intimate seasons I have ever had with God, my Father, my Protector, my Jesus.

Noonie Fugler has been cancer-free for more than six years.

11

The Diligence of Knowing Christ

As you may have gathered, knowing Christ is more about heart and attitude than it is about action. But it does take effort, and that's what this chapter is all about.

This effort doesn't *define* our relationship with Jesus (performance Christianity), but this effort *deepens* our relationship with him.

Five of our grandchildren are with us this week. Our house is one big party. The kids are wonderful, well-behaved and responsible. But with our once-orderly home packed with children from ages 2-12, life is vastly different than we knew a week ago.

I've learned that the discipline of knowing Jesus is one that takes intentionality. With five grandchildren around, I can't just retreat to the patio for time with God. At least one child follows me. She wants to be with grandpa. That's a good illustration of how we should pursue God, but that's a message for another time.

Even when I do manage to stow away somewhere, noise from the distance flows into my ears and mind. My train of thought or my prayer is gradually interrupted.

I've tried rising early to sneak in a good quiet time, but 5:00 am is too much for me to bear. At that hour, I doze off more than I pray.

Young parents reading this story are smiling. You're telling me that this is the real world. This is the battle you face every day in finding the bandwidth to develop your intimate relationship with Jesus.

I get it. Memories of my early parenting days flash into my mind. I fought fatigue, irritability, noise and confusion like you do. It's hard to rest in the Lord when little ones are constantly pressing in.

The biggest lesson I've learned this week is that I have to be diligent to know Jesus. It doesn't just happen. It's hard work, just like any relationship. And this is the most important relationship of all.

When the grandkids go home next week, the pressures won't disappear. They'll just be replaced with new ones. Demands at work. Commitments at church. Time pressures and deadlines that come at me on a regular basis.

Raising small children can be one of the most difficult seasons to navigate when you're trying to deepen your relationship with Jesus. The noise and commotion wear you out. The kids' mere presence in the room interrupts your solitude with God.

On the other end of the spectrum, there's the season of caring for aging parents or an ailing spouse. The constant demands give you little time to retreat with Jesus. It's even hard to *think* about your relationship with him.

> Every stage of life presents its challenges to knowing Jesus.

Every stage of life presents its challenges to knowing Jesus. And within those stages are seasons that present seemingly impossible scenarios.

Tenacity is required when it comes to knowing Christ. The apostle Paul overcame many things that interfered with knowing his Savior. He didn't raise small children, but he knew what it was like for life itself to edge out his "Jesus time."

He sat in prison in chains. Yet, in the hardship of a cold prison cell, with no scrolls of Scripture or writing materials, he grew in his relationship with Jesus. He learned to commune with the Lord.

He was shipwrecked at least three times. In all the terror and commotion, he grew in knowing Christ. Throughout these times of survival, he clung to Jesus. He made time for the relationship. I don't know how, but he must have. His relationship was so solid he wasn't sidelined for the future.

Opposition hounded him. The more he preached, the more he drew the ire of Jewish leaders. In his testimony to King Agrippa, Paul said, "I preached that they should repent and turn to God and demonstrate their repentance by their deeds. That is why some Jews seized me in the temple courts and tried to kill me" (Acts 26:20-21 NIV).

Paul needed the grace of God to stay spiritually healthy. So do you. Your day-to-day survival is dependent upon your relationship with Christ. As the battle grows more intense, you need Jesus more. While you depend on Christ, be diligent to practice habits that will help you know him and flourish. Believe me, I would have done things differently 30 years ago if I knew what I know now. And I would have avoided destructive seasons in my life.

Above all, protect your Jesus time. Whatever you do, get regular time alone with Jesus. It's vital. It may seem impossible, but that makes it even more important. You will have to go to great lengths to make sure you have quiet times as frequently as possible. Fight for this time. Call in reinforcements, like someone to watch your kids, to help you make this happen. Be different than the average Christian who just lets life happen. Not because they don't care, but because they are overwhelmed.

Here are two elements that will make your time with Jesus fruitful for your relationship.

Have a Plan

Just as you plan the most important activities in your life and family, plan time to get to know Jesus. Without a plan, you'll drift back into confusion. Write the plan down. Put it on stone tablets. Or a Post-it Note. Make it official. Tell your kids and spouse.

This is a tangible way to pursue knowing Jesus.
- ***When*** will you meet with God each day? Routine and consistency are your friends.
- ***Where*** will you meet with God? Having a familiar place becomes your special place. When I sink into *the* chair in the morning, I tend to go into "seeking Jesus" mode. Find a place where you can stow away with Jesus.
- ***What*** will you do in your time with God? You could study a Gospel chapter, revisit a favorite Psalm, be still before God and enjoy his presence or dedicate the time to pray for each member of your family. There are many quiet time guides available.
- ***How*** will you protect this time? Set boundaries—such as not defaulting to your phone until after you meet with God, getting up a little earlier while it's quiet or asking family members not to interrupt you.

Include these things in your plan. Be as specific as possible. Then prepare to make adjustments, because you'll need to.

Have a Purpose

Your time with Jesus is so valuable that you want to maximize it. These minutes together will determine how you approach the day. Your quiet time is your anchor. It's where you connect with the Living God. Moses' face was shining when he came down from the mountain after meeting with God. I believe our countenance should reflect the Savior we've met with.

While your plan is *what* you'll do in your time together, your *purpose* is the *reason* for getting together with Jesus. By now, you can guess what I'll say that purpose should be—to *know* him. However, be more specific, depending on your season of life. Your purpose might be healing, attaining wisdom for a big decision, reconciliation with God, rest, reflection, praise, crying, strength for the day or some other timely objective.

Knowing Jesus isn't a formula. It's a personal, dynamic experience with the living God. Although you plan your Jesus time, you can't control it. It belongs to God. He will live inside this plan and make it a special experience for this stage of your life. Above all, be diligent to protect this most important relationship.

Your Story

- Think about all the interruptions you face when you try to have quality time with Jesus. Make a mental list. How can you overcome them with a plan and purpose? Write down your thoughts.

- How can you keep your inner Pharisee from making this time with God another thing to check off your to-do list rather than an experience of knowing Christ more deeply?

- Make a commitment to guard your time with God.

[If you need structure for your quiet time, I recommend you start through the exercises in **Appendix A: Exercises in Knowing Jesus**].

12

How to Make Progress in Knowing Jesus

Knowing Jesus is the most intriguing, exciting, fascinating and fulfilling experience life has to offer. Or should I say *God* has to offer?

Praise God that knowing Jesus never results in the shallowness that the world brings us. In this success-bound world, we marry the spouse, get the home, land the job, make money, achieve milestones and retire with big bucks in the bank. We're reaching out for fulfillment every step of the way, but the world never fully delivers on it. Deep within, we want more than that. Only Christ can satisfy.

Richness in knowing Jesus requires simple habits inspired by a simple attitude. I'll show you what I mean.

As believers, we're caught between the lures of the world and the call of Jesus. Which do we want more? I have to admit, I like comfort. I'm drawn to it, but the satisfaction is only temporary.

I seem to raise the bar to continue feeling comfortable. What satisfied last year doesn't do it this year.

What's your lure of the world? How is it pulling you away from Christ?

This is a battle we'll face for the rest of our lives. It's called spiritual warfare, the flesh against the spirit. "For the flesh desires what is contrary to the Spirit, and the Spirit what is contrary to the flesh. They are in conflict with each other, so that you are not to do whatever you want" (Galatians 5:17 NIV).

This fight is also called the new, reborn me against the old me. "You were taught, with regard to your former way of life, to put off your old self, which is being corrupted by its deceitful desires; to be made new in the attitude of your minds; and to put on the new self, created to be like God in true righteousness and holiness" (Ephesians 4:22-24 NIV).

I can have the best day of my life on Monday, but slide into the spiritual ditch on Tuesday. Then on Wednesday, a passage of Scripture connects with me in the morning and stays with me all day. I feel alive, close to Jesus. I'm joyful, hopeful, strong. Circumstances don't rock me. Thursday rolls around and it rolls *me* around. I'm short-tempered, sad, stale and low. The closeness to Christ I felt the day before escaped out my bedroom window overnight.

What happened?

Jesus is still the same. And my circumstances haven't changed much. But my relationship with my Savior has gone south. The difference is me.

I've learned not to evaluate my walk with God from one day to the next. We're emotional creatures, which means we have ups and downs. How I feel about my relationship with Jesus doesn't always reflect reality.

My emotional highs can be circumstantial, as can be my emotional lows. Or I may not have an explanation at all. That's alright.

I want to encourage you to be free in your relationship with your loving Savior. Not every day is going to be a home run emotionally. If it were, you'd be exhausted running around the bases. There are days that are calm, even rocky. That's the norm of life.

Look at life in seasons. How's your relationship with Jesus this season? It might be marked by events. Your first year of marriage, the first child going off to college, starting a new job, death in the family, moving to a new location, assuming new responsibilities at church or a number of other things.

My wife and I moved to North Carolina a few years ago for me to start a new ministry job. It was a season with a marked beginning and an undefined ending. The season began when we sold our house in Colorado. Life hit a frantic pace as we prepared for the move four weeks later. We emptied the house, loaded everything in the moving pod, spent a few weeks living in our kids' basement, left my job, drove across the country, then moved frantically into our new home. We were exhausted. Let me add an adjective to that—*exhilaratingly* exhausted. Our emotions were high as we prepared for the next season.

That transition birthed a renewed relationship with Jesus. God deepened my understanding and experience of knowing Christ. It was so dramatic that I wrote seven devotionals over the next year. My heart was overflowing and spilled out my fingertips onto the keyboard.

What drew me into that renewed relationship? Did I hear a great sermon that launched me into the new season? Attend an awesome retreat? Read a life-changing book? Meet with a friend for prayer every day?

> **That transition birthed a renewed relationship with Jesus. God deepened my understanding and experience of knowing Christ.**

No. None of those things.

It was directly related to the time I spent with Jesus. Not that I started getting up at 4 a.m. for my devotions or went off to a monastery to be alone with my Savior. Remember, we were in transition, so a regular schedule wasn't possible.

I met with God every day. I sought fulfillment in my relationship with him, not in the achievements or distractions of the world. Perhaps leaving the stability of our home, family and friends, as well as saying good-bye to my old job, put me in an attitude of need. Needing God.

When we discover that we need God, we lean into him. I picture Jesus at the last supper with his disciples. They reclined at the table, one head resting on the chest of the next. John, most likely, was the most fortunate one. He laid his head on the chest of Jesus. This intimate visual comes to mind when I think of needing Jesus.

Our loving Savior beckons us to lay our head on his chest, unrushed, enjoying a meal and talking about life. Oh, how this is a picture of a loving relationship with Jesus. Not for a last supper, but for every meal. Every day. Every season. Imagine the conversations we can have with Jesus.

Rest your head on the chest of Jesus. I believe I did that for months in our season of transition. I was so drawn to Jesus I carved out extra time to write about him. For you, it may be singing praises or hymns to God, quietly listening to him or reading the gospels in greater depth. Dine with Jesus.

What an adventure! You get to spend time with Jesus every day. As often as you'd like. You ask him questions, share your deepest prayers, read the Word about his life. As I say about my quiet times with God, "There are no rules." It's about relationship.

When you come to the Lord with the *attitude* that you want to know him, you *will*. You'll look back on those seasons, as I just did, and realize that you know Jesus more deeply and personally. Your love relationship will grow. For me, I've built on that season, some five years down the road. I know Jesus better. It has affected my life with a steadiness in my faith and a sensitivity to God. I see the Lord in things where I had missed him before.

Jesus offers you an intimate meal with him.

With that in mind, consider his words in Revelation 3:20 (NIV). Often used to lead someone to salvation, this verse is for a lifetime with Jesus. "Here I am! I stand at the door and knock. If anyone hears my voice and opens the door, I will come in and eat with that person, and they with me."

Your Story

When you know Jesus more, you'll want to spend more time with him. Feed that desire. Do it in other times of the day and settings.

You may go for walks at lunch, praying to Jesus, or singing to him. Fill your mind and heart with praise music. Listen to the audio Bible. Journal at night. Whatever works for you, do it. There are no rules. You're in for an adventure!

13

Trials Drive us to Know Jesus

The momentum was building. Over a few months, I'd dropped almost 20 pounds. My goal was in sight. Just three pounds to go. Up and down I went over the next two months, creeping closer to the prized weight, then sliding back up a couple pounds. I couldn't crack that barrier. But I knew I'd make it soon. My weight was like a yo-yo, dancing a couple inches above my goal. I was determined.

Losing the excess baggage added another blessing. I was swifter than I had been in years. My running time for 5K dropped dramatically. I had carved off a minute from my average time. I felt five years younger. At least that's what my times indicated.

At 63, I was a great runner again. At least in my eyes. To keep it in perspective, my same-age buddy was a minute-per mile faster than me. Still, I was feeling pretty good about myself. Was I getting prideful, knowing that most men my age don't take up running as a hobby?

If so, that pride came crashing down in a matter of days. The first mishap slammed me as I was running around the tiny track at the gym. Coming around a turn and starting on the short straightaway, I felt something pop just below my right ankle on the outside of my foot. Thinking it was a cramp, I tried to keep running. But after only two steps, I almost collapsed. I hobbled off the track dumbfounded. This came out of nowhere.

It was definitely not a cramp. Looking back, I suspect I pulled a ligament in my foot, just enough to let me walk but keep me from running. Even while walking, the dull pain was a reminder of my humanness. Were my running days over?

Discouragement set in quickly. I'd lost the thing that energized me, as well as helped me conquer my weight challenge. Like most runners, there's an emotional high that comes from the exertion. No more happy hormones for me. I figured I'd take up cycling instead.

That incident faded into oblivion a few days later. A much more dramatic catastrophe struck my body. My first mistake was competing while still injured. I knew it in the back of my mind, but couldn't resist engaging in whiffle ball, driveway hockey and basketball with my son and grandkids on Christmas Day.

Protecting my foot, I didn't run. But moving slower than normal is a recipe for disaster when you're competing in sports. Even recreationally.

My son rolled the basketball hoop fixture into place at the end of the driveway. It was a big, heavy base supporting and stabilizing a thick metal pole, backboard and hoop.

Minutes into the two-on-two contest, I found myself open near the basket, reaching up for a pass. Careful not to hurt my foot, I stepped slowly backwards. That's when disaster struck. My foot hit the base and I fell sideways, my hands still reaching up for the pass. Thankfully, I was hardly moving to begin with, so my fall was in slow-motion. But very real.

Totally out of control, my right leg twisted in the wrong direction on the way down. My hip slammed onto the top of the base. I rolled off, with my hands trying to break the fall onto the gravel street. That maneuver must have done some good, because my head didn't hit as hard as it could have. I felt a sharp pain in my temple where the stones punctured my skin. My hands were on fire from the fall and my hip was throbbing from the impact.

I came to a stop on my back, tightly clenching every muscle and joint possible. Quietly, I moaned for the pain to stop.

My family ran towards me quickly. All they could see was blood pouring out of my head onto the street. In reality, it was just a small cut near my eyebrow, but no one was able to tell at the time. The neighbor was a doctor in residency. Her husband was the one who had thrown me the pass. Thankfully, she was at home and led the triage efforts. The bleeding stopped but the pain didn't.

My head was fine. My hands still burned. My elbow was scraped up. But my leg was the big problem. I had torn my groin muscle, right at the point that it reached my waist. I felt like I had done the splits. With one leg.

My son helped me up and I almost collapsed. No position relieved the groin pain. Any slight pressure or twisting was unbearable. Finally, the family was able to round up an ancient rolling office chair from the garage, which became my only comfortable place for the next three days of our stay. I wheeled around the house with one leg.

Merry Christmas.

Physical pain is one thing. Emotional distress is another.

> **Physical pain is one thing. Emotional distress is another.**

I know my injury wasn't severe, compared to what so many others have endured. In fact, one of my best friends had an angiogram the day after my fall, discovering that his heart was functioning at only 25% capacity.

I recovered slowly, not taking another running step for two months. I have to admit that I failed the test of emotional strength, rattled by the effects of the injury. To make things worse, my other leg was attacked one week later by a guy named Sciatica. Both legs were in severe pain, forcing me to use a walker for two weeks. I was a basket case.

Times like these are opportunities to know Jesus in the deepest ways. Paul discovered it over and over again in his shipwrecks, beatings and abandonments. He drew closer to Christ.

I wrestled with God for the next several days. My journaling revealed my disappointment in not being able to achieve the goals

I had set for the new year. My vision was crushed. I had priorities. Gone. Ministry things to accomplish. On hold. Books to write. Nope. Now I was cheated out of those things.

I was shipwrecked and didn't like it. More than that, I chose not to see God in it. I complained, feeling sorry for myself.

Then there was a turning point. It's recorded in my journal. I prayed, "Lord, help me rid myself of the world and absorb your ways. Your thoughts. Your heart. Please, Lord Jesus."

This was my cry to Jesus to know him.

The next day, I read these verses:

"Delight yourself in the Lord, and he will give you the desires of your heart. Commit your way to the Lord; trust in him, and he will act" (Psalms 37:4-5 ESV).

"The steps of a man are established by the Lord, when he delights in his way" (Psalms 37:23 ESV).

Delight in the Lord! That's the key.

I was dumping on the Lord rather than delighting in him.

This immediate shift changed my entire mindset, emotions and life with Christ. In my suffering, I asked for God to teach me so I would trust him more. I was drawing near to Christ.

I ended my day's journal with these words, "I lift my voice in praise to you today. For your glory. And honor. And praise. Amen."

My journey to know the Christ of the cross intensified over the next several months. Then God tested me again.

If we let trials drive us *towards* our Savior, we will not only know Christ more fully, we'll become a more mature believer, conformed to the image of Jesus.

James said it this way: "Consider it pure joy, my brothers and sisters, whenever you face trials of many kinds, because you know that the testing of your faith produces perseverance. Let perseverance finish its work so that you may be mature and complete, not lacking anything" (James 1:2-4 NIV).

Your Story

When you feel distant from God, it could be the result of the wrong response to trials. (In my situation, I complained and felt sorry for myself).

- Reflect on a trial in your life. Which one comes to mind? Did you let it drive you towards Christ or away? You had the choice to draw near to the Lord, just as I did.

Here are some passages to reflect on that have the power to change your attitude, drawing you to Jesus in times of trial.

"Praise be to the God and Father of our Lord Jesus Christ, the Father of compassion and the God of all comfort, who comforts us in all our troubles, so that we can comfort those in any trouble with the comfort we ourselves receive from God" (2 Corinthians 1:3-4 NIV).

"For I am convinced that neither death nor life, neither angels nor demons, neither the present nor the future, nor any powers, neither height nor depth, nor anything else in all creation, will be able to separate us from the love of God that is in Christ Jesus our Lord" (Romans 8:38-39 NIV).

"The LORD is my rock, my fortress and my deliverer; my God is my rock, in whom I take refuge, my shield and the horn of my salvation, my stronghold" (Psalm 18:2 NIV).

"Truly my soul finds rest in God; my salvation comes from him. Truly he is my rock and my salvation; he is my fortress, I will never be shaken" (Psalm 62:1-2 NIV).

Parker's Story

Burnout to Build Up

I asked myself a simple question as I lay in the hospital bed in the summer of 2021. I had been brought to Emergency by my twin sister, who had threatened me with death if I didn't go.

By the time I was seen by a doctor and the chaos of the day had calmed, I asked myself in the darkness of the room, "How did I end up here?" Lying there, I pondered what had happened. I had just returned from a writer's conference and vacation in South Dakota and Wyoming, so I should have been rested.

But that day, when I got back from the vacation, I took a long, four-hour nap until mid-afternoon, when it was time to host my podcast where I interview Christian authors. I had been pushing hard and it had grown to 10-13 shows a month. During the show that day, I fell asleep. Live on air.

Thankfully, it was only a micro-nap and I woke up a second later. But it was the first time I had ever fallen asleep on a podcast. "That micro-nap was an anomaly," I thought.

The next day, I could barely get out of bed. It was a struggle to walk. I felt disoriented and detached. Was it just jet lag?

Then came the moment when I couldn't move at all. My strength was gone. Vanished. After my twin coerced me, I ended up in the hospital, taking a battery of tests to find out what was wrong.

As I lay there, I heard the Spirit tell me, "You're not doing ministry. You're just creating content."

At first, I didn't understand that rebuke. I had been doing this podcast for years. But I had lost sight that my podcast was meant to be a ministry and a relationship builder with like-minded authors. I had become a slave to creating content.

I had burned out even when I didn't know I had burned out. I was a one-woman show.

Laying there in the hospital bed, I cried and realized that I had forgotten why the Lord had called me to podcast. To be a ministry, a support, and an advocate for Christian authors. To use the podcast to reach Christian readers.

So, I packed up the podcast. I thought that was the end of it. No more podcast.

God wanted me to focus on building and strengthening my relationship with him. Not just making content for him. So I spent the next three months doing that.

After time off and restructuring my schedule, God graciously returned me to my podcast. Now I do it at a much more normal pace, once or twice a week. I have help, too. And my sanity has returned.

I'm grateful for the breakdown. That's when the Lord built me up again.

Parker J. Cole is an outstanding fiction author and host of the Write Stuff podcast.

14

The Presence of Jesus in Our Pain

Pain has a way of humbling us. It seems that I needed a lot of humbling the year of my Christmas tumble.

After overcoming the setback of my injury, I decided to hit the running trail exactly two months later. I was dying to get out on the street and run like Forest Gump, but I was hesitant to reinjure myself. Finally, the day came when I said, "Let's do it!"

I was in Marseille, France, of all places. On an early afternoon, I stepped out of the hotel in my running clothes and embarked on a one-mile run. Despite one of my slowest times, I made it pain-free! That's all that mattered. I called it my "Marseille Miracle Mile." Somehow, I felt whole again.

Life was good. I was energized and hit the road running three times a week. It was my mental and emotional therapy.

Months passed and my times were getting better. Other things in my life, family and ministry began coming together, too. I felt blessed, covered by God's favor.

For 4th of July weekend, Noonie and I went on a vacation to the ocean, our favorite place to go. With masks in hand (Coronavirus was prevalent), we enjoyed a country drive through North and South Carolina to the shoreline. The water was warm, the beach wasn't crowded and we settled into a hotel in Myrtle Beach for the week.

Until I was humbled again. On the third day, I pulled a lower-back muscle, lifting groceries out of the car. This star runner had been slowed by a simple physical task. So much for running on the beach, taking long walks with Noonie and biking together around the lovely coastal town. I was stuck. And discouraged.

But I sucked it up and used the time to slow down, sit on the shore and spend mornings in the hotel room, writing "exceptional" spiritual truths for my next book. But the Lord had other plans that took me to a deeper valley.

The next night, I bent over too quickly in the hotel room. My sciatica exploded, sending the worst pain of my life throughout my left side. I couldn't move. I stood there in agony. Sitting wasn't possible. Sweat poured down my face as the pain riddled my body. Then came the nausea. Was I going to faint? I asked Noonie to hold me so I didn't slam into something if I blacked out.

Somehow, I made it five feet to the bed. With increasing torture in every movement, I lowered myself to the mattress and eased onto my back. It was the only position that didn't cause shooting pain. By then, my body was traumatized. I lay there, still in shock over what had just happened.

I was horizontal for the next 48 hours, not able to turn an inch without sharp pain. The ocean was 50 yards away out the window, but I never saw it again.

We reached out to my doctor for a solution and he came through with strong pain meds. No effect at all. I was completely disabled. Noonie was so worried she called one of our best friends in California, also a doctor, for help. After sizing up the situation, he delivered the news that I must go the ER, and it would be by ambulance. Humble me further!

Within an hour, the paramedics safely slid me off the bed, onto the gurney, transported me down the elevator and then to the hospital, where they lifted me by the sheets onto the emergency room bed.

It took a powerful pain pill and two doses of morphine to enable me to sit up, stand up, get into my car and have Noonie drive us three hours home in the middle of the night. I have to say, I was in a pretty good mood. No pain now!

I'm a baby. When I'm in pain, it captures all my attention and dulls my spiritual senses. As much as I try to concentrate on the Lord and engage in prayer, I'm not the guy who can connect deeply with God at times like this. Honestly, I can be selfish. I think about me.

> I'm not the guy who can connect deeply with God at times like this.

This was a moment of truth. All the things I had spouted about God, knowing Christ and having a deep personal relationship with him—did they work in real life? Or were they words on a page and myths in my mind?

Nearly two weeks after the accident, still far from healed, I had one of my most intimate experiences with God. Early one morning, I sat alone with him with my Bible open to a passage that he had shown me a few days earlier:

"Yes, my soul, find rest in God; my hope comes from him.
Truly he is my rock and my salvation;
he is my fortress, I will not be shaken.
My salvation and my honor depend on God;
he is my mighty rock, my refuge.
Trust in him at all times, you people;
pour out your hearts to him,
for God is our refuge" (Psalm 62:5-8 NIV).

I began to tear up. Then cry. Then sob. It was just Jesus and me on our back porch, the sun rising through the trees. I vividly remembered the physical pain I had experienced. My cries to God grew deeper. I had stored so much emotional pain and now everything was hitting me hard.

Jesus accepted my tears. I felt his love.

I had felt punished by my injury, but Jesus turned that around as I sat with him in tears. The injuries were a *gift* so I would know him in a more personal and deeper way than I had ever thought or experienced. Months before, I had told God that I wanted to know the Christ of the cross just as Paul did (Philippians 3:8, 10). Pain was the path to that reward. To that depth of relationship.

This is new territory for me. I'm just cracking open the door to this world. My self-sufficiency had been dashed in a moment, reducing me to a man who could do nothing for himself. Two weeks earlier I had been running three miles three times a week. Then on my back, I was helpless. I have so much more to learn from that experience.

The journey to know Christ continues. He is developing me in light of eternity. He has an eternal view that I need to know. I hope my experience of pain has changed my life forever.

I hope, too, that my story speaks into yours.

Your Story

- What are some qualities of God's character that you experience in your times of physical pain, illness or disease? What are qualities you have a hard time experiencing?

In Appendix A, there are 10 exercises exploring several identities of Jesus. These will help you as you seek to know Jesus better in your pain.

Jim's Story

When the Pain Doesn't Go Away

I played tennis aggressively for 40 years. I coached Little League for nearly 20 years and was a Boy Scout leader for over a decade. I also ran my own company.

Then, 12 years ago, it all started—shooting pains in my lower back and down my legs.

The orthopedic surgeon recommended taking large doses of Advil. That worked for a while. Then he sent me to a pain management doctor. After dozens of treatments of epidural and cortisone shots, he used radio frequency ablation (RFA) for six years. That's where they stick needles in the areas of pain, sending an electric current for two minutes to cauterize the nerve endings. It wasn't fun.

While experiencing some temporary relief, the pain always returned stronger than before.

I was in such agony that I was bent over, using a cane and unable to do much. On a scale of 1 to 10, I was living at 7 to 8. I prayed continually for God to ease my pain.

The time had come to yield to surgery. The doctor fused L-3, L-4, and L-5 during a five-hour operation. For two years I felt healthy again. But then, further down my spine, the pain returned. Off I went to the pain management doctor for four more years of RFA treatments. Another back surgery followed.

It has been five months since then. Now my pain level maxes out at a 5. But there are moments when it is severe.

Throughout all this ordeal, I have maintained my faith in the Lord. I read and reread some favorite passages that comfort me.

- Romans 5:3-5: "Not only that, but we rejoice in our sufferings, knowing that suffering produces endurance and endurance produces character, and character produces hope."

- James 1:2-4: "Count it all joy, my brothers, when you meet trials of various kinds, for you know that the testing of your faith produces steadfastness. And let steadfastness have its full effect, that you may be perfect and complete, lacking in nothing."
- Romans 8:18: "For I consider that the sufferings of the present time are not worth comparing with the glory that is to be revealed to us."

Admittedly, this life of pain gets to me mentally and emotionally. But with the pain comes the realization that I'm not invincible, can't solve all my problems by myself, and that I'm physically weak.

Above all, I know that I need God's help to get me through the day. I thank him for every new day he gives me, praying for the strength to endure. My back pain has truly brought me so much closer to our Lord. He has given me such lasting peace.

This new relationship with Jesus, forged through serious back pain, has inspired me to seek ways to serve him and others. I will do so until he calls me home.

I thank the Lord for my beloved wife of more than 50 years. During the day, she encourages me to take time to rest. She understands and puts up with my curt responses when she knows the pain has finally dampened my attitude. She is my "angel."

If you experience the depth of pain that I do, turn to the Lord. He will give you the means to get through another day. Your attitude is a choice. Rather than being bitter (which aggravates the pain), choose to be thankful. Spend time in prayer and studying the Bible. Be a blessing to those around you. God loves you and wants the best for you. You and I must trust in him!

Jim Van Houten is a retired financial planner and author of several books on personal finance.

15

Knowing Jesus as the Way, the Truth and the Life

"I am the way, the truth and the life" (John 14:6 ESV).

That pretty much sums up who Jesus is. There's so much to explore in this verse as we grow deep in our relationship with the Savior.

The Way

When you came to know Christ, you confessed that he was the way to God. The *only* way. He was your onramp to an incredible journey with him. Not only *was* he the way when you first acknowledged it, but he is still the way. His role hasn't changed.

When you're struggling in your faith, Jesus is the way back. Don't try anything else. He is *the* way.

Why do we try spiritual gymnastics when we're distant from the Lord? The Pharisee within us opts for legalism, Christian behavior without heart. We go into the mode of trying to earn

God's approval so we can revive our relationship with him. We might score a 10 on the rings or high beam in our magnificent performance, but inside we're still empty.

I think we choose this route because we're conditioned, in our sinful state, to fix things on our own. Yet, our walk with Christ is just the opposite. He has already fixed things. We just need to turn to him. He is the way. It's that simple.

Instead of doing good works to try to make things right or earn his favor, walk towards Jesus and fall into his arms. He doesn't want your money, service, good works, extra Bible study, church attendance or devoted prayer. Get right with him first by pouring out your heart. Good works will follow, not as a way to earn his favor but out of gratitude for him.

Jesus is the way to eternal life but he is also the way to the abundant life. He says, "The thief comes only to steal and kill and destroy; I came so that they would have life, and have it abundantly" (John 10:10 NASB). Or as the NIV puts it, life "to the full." The enemy, Satan, wants to destroy you by wrapping you up in endless favor-seeking works. Jesus is the good shepherd who offers a full, abundant life in himself. What a gift!

The work has already been done for us to have a full relationship with God. That's what the cross is all about. Complete and total reconciliation. Long before he went to Calvary, Jesus told his disciples why he came. "I am the good shepherd. The good shepherd lays down his life for the sheep" (John 10:11 NIV). My friend, a reconciled relationship with God *is* the abundant life.

> **My friend, a reconciled relationship with God *is* the abundant life.**

As a believer, you live in a state of grace. Enter into *the way* every single day. Enter into Jesus. Don't be deceived by thinking you have to earn your relationship with him today. He is the way to the full, continuously reconciled life. It's a life of freedom! What a great promise.

> ***Are you anxious?*** Jesus is the way, offering peace. "And the peace of God, which surpasses all understanding, will guard your hearts and your minds in Christ Jesus" (Philippians 4:7 ESV).

Are you fearful? Jesus is the way, offering courage. "For God gave us a spirit not of fear but of power and love and self-control" (2 Timothy 1:7 ESV).

Bitter? Jesus is the way, offering forgiveness. "Be kind and compassionate to one another, forgiving each other, just as in Christ God forgave you" (Ephesians 4:32 NIV).

Broken? Jesus is the way, offering healing. "The LORD is close to the brokenhearted and saves those who are crushed in spirit" (Psalm 34:18 NIV).

Confused? Jesus is the way, offering wisdom. "If any of you lacks wisdom, you should ask God, who gives generously to all without finding fault, and it will be given to you" (James 1:5 NIV).

Discouraged? Jesus is the way, offering hope. "Therefore we do not lose heart. Though outwardly we are wasting away, yet inwardly we are being renewed day by day. For our light and momentary troubles are achieving for us an eternal glory that far outweighs them all. So we fix our eyes not on what is seen, but on what is unseen, since what is seen is temporary, but what is unseen is eternal" (2 Corinthians 4:16-18 NIV).

If you have peace, courage, forgiveness, healing, wisdom and hope, these add up to the abundant life. It's what Jesus meant when he said he came that we might have life to the full. He provides what our hearts truly long for. Not surface desires like money, fame and status, but the deep things that make us whole.

Jesus is the way. For salvation and for our daily lives as believers.

The Truth

I was a sneaky kid growing up. I think that's the nature of most children. One of my grand adventures was to make stealth trips to the grocery store a mile away, running behind the houses so I wouldn't be spotted if my parents drove by. I did the best I could to stay under the cover of homes, bushes and trees. My reward was the purchase of my favorite, individually wrapped Brach's candy.

I'd run my sneaky route in reverse to bring the candy home and hide it.

You have your sneaky stories to tell, too. Feel free to email me with any confessions! I think every kid is sneaky to some degree, pushing the envelope. Unfortunately, the stakes are higher in each stage of life. Our sneakiness can get us into big trouble. No confession offered here.

To keep our kids on track to be the wonderful citizens that they are today (Ha, proud parent remark), my wife used to use one brilliant line that I still marvel at today. When she suspected that our kids were hiding something or not telling us the real story, she would say, "Tell me like Jesus saw it."

Talk about cutting to the chase, that line did it. And it worked. Our kids would come clean.

"Oh, alright. I hit Tommy first."

I guess that's what it means to put the fear of God into them. Try it on your kids and see what happens.

When facing the One who is the embodiment of truth, we are cut to the core when we hide something. How can we stand before Jesus, look him in the eye, and not be confronted with any sin in our lives? He doesn't even need to say anything. If we understand even a fraction of who Jesus is, we marvel at his truth.

In David's masterful writing in Psalm 139, he is completely transparent before God, concluding with:

"Search me, God, and know my heart; test me and know my anxious thoughts. See if there is any offensive way in me, and lead me in the way everlasting" (Psalm 139:23-24 NIV).

As our way to salvation, Jesus also reveals the *truth* about God. We come to salvation informed about him. It doesn't end there. Jesus is the truth we follow in our ongoing walk of faith.

Paul said, "I am crucified with Christ; and it is no longer I who live, but it is **Christ who lives in me" (Galatians 2:20 ESV)**. As a Christian, Jesus the truth lives inside you. He supplies you with all the knowledge you need to live out your faith. Call on him for truth. *The* truth.

You possess the truth. The truth of Christ inside you does battle with Satan, the father of lies. You're fully equipped to face Satan and this fallen world. A world that is strewn with lies.

Jesus, the living Word, is absolutely critical for you to live out the truth. The book of John opens with the beautiful exposition of the Word and Jesus being one, culminating in verse 14, "The Word became flesh and made his dwelling among us" (NIV).

All of God's Word, Scripture, came to life in Christ. This same Christ is the truth. God's Word is truth.

In the Gospels, how inspiring to read the *spoken* truth, the words of Christ. Every word is truth, coming from the One who is 100% truth.

When Jesus announced that he was the truth, he had more in mind than the span of his earthly existence. He was the living Word that transcended his time on earth. Jesus was there with the Father at the beginning of creation as the truth. "In the beginning was the Word, and the Word was with God, and the Word was God. He was with God in the beginning" (John 1:1-2 NIV).

Jesus is the eternal truth. He and the Word are one and the same. The Word is eternal truth.

Read the Word and you'll get to know Jesus better. Internalize the Word and you'll distinguish between lies and truth. You'll see life "as Jesus sees it."

Do you want to know the truth each and every day, successfully battling against the lies this world and Satan throw at you? Know the Word. And know Jesus.

The Life

The powerful nine-word statement we've been exploring ends with "life."

"I am the way, the truth and the life." –Jesus

There's not a human on this earth who doesn't long for life. At least we start that way. We seek life in our families, marriage, jobs, income, home, luxuries, goals and purpose, freedom and recreation. We try just about everything to experience life.

Yet, John opens his Gospel with the clear statement, "In him was life, and that life was the light of all mankind" (John 1:4 NIV).

Our quest for life is no different than when Jesus spoke that short sentence. People in those days sought significance, purpose, power, contentment and satisfaction. So do we. They pursued wealth, comfort, sex, property, marriage, family and personal achievement or position. So do we. We just have more choices to try to gain these things. To find life. We have far more things calling to us with the promise of life. People move from one attraction to the next, from cradle to grave.

It's not only non-Christians who pursue empty promises of life. Hold up the mirror. I'm standing right next to you, guilty of pursuing life outside of Christ. I especially enjoy comfort. I also like people's approval. Work is a big draw for satisfaction. Financial security pulls me in. Then there's baseball. Whew! It's a daily battle. I get sucked into the world. Media floods our minds and souls. We become conformed to the world rather than conformed to Christ. It happens over time and we eventually normalize the things of the world. In Christ's eyes, these substitutes rot quickly.

> We become conformed to the world rather than conformed to Christ. It happens over time and we eventually normalize the things of the world.

Before his conversion, Paul pursued life with all the gusto he had. His religion was at his core. As Saul, he was a man of religious position and power as a well-educated Pharisee. From the secular side as a Roman and the spiritual side as a Jew, he had life and no one could take it away.

Until Jesus did.

Saul's sudden transformation to a Christ-follower compelled him to leave "life" behind for real life in Christ. This about-face was so radical that, many years later, he said, "What is more, I consider everything a loss because of the surpassing worth of knowing Christ Jesus my Lord, for whose sake I have lost all things. I consider them garbage, that I may gain Christ" (Philippians 3:8 NIV).

Life as he knew it before conversion was garbage compared to the life he knew in knowing Christ.

Why do we pursue garbage instead of Christ, the one who *is* life?

Is garbage too strong a word? How can our jobs, spouse, kids, home, position, health, bank accounts and goals be considered garbage? God has given them to us as gifts, right? James 1:17 says, "Every good and perfect gift is from above, coming down from the Father of the heavenly lights" (NIV).

Yes, we have been bestowed with good gifts. So had Paul. His position, lineage, home and all other blessings were gifts from God. He was devoutly religious, yet he sure missed it spiritually when it concerned Christ. The Damascus Road visit by Jesus was a life-changer. Christ became his greatest gift of all. In comparison, he saw all his other gifts as garbage.

The point is this. There is nothing more valuable than Jesus. We can't compare knowing Christ to anything else without viewing those things as trash, garbage. When we fall in love with Jesus, everything this world has to offer fades in significance. We can enjoy the good gifts God gives us from heaven, but we can't put them ahead of Christ. That would be worship. These temporal things are for our enjoyment; we honor and glorify Christ as the only one we worship.

> When we fall in love with Jesus, everything this world has to offer fades in significance.

Oh, how I wish we would welcome Christ to be at the center of our lives every single day. Out of him flows genuine life.

With Christ at the center, we can't help but be concerned with the souls of men, women and children around us. We will have compassion on the poor and downtrodden—and do something about it. We will turn our backs on sin to face our Savior in his holiness. We will cry over our cities. Our prayer lives will be wrapped up in Christ. We will embrace humility, as Christ did, becoming more like him. Joy will flow from us because Christ lives at the center of our hearts.

And this is just the beginning of the life Christ promises. The LIFE that Jesus offers you is summed up in these verses, "But the fruit of the Spirit is love, joy, peace, patience, kindness, goodness, faithfulness, gentleness, self-control." Galatians 5:22-23 ESV)

Who wouldn't want all that?

Once again, we turn to Paul for a life lesson. He was beaten, shipwrecked and nearly killed many times. He was starved, cold, wet and persecuted to the max. Yet, because he knew Christ he was able to say, "I have learned to be content whatever the circumstances. I know what it is to be in need, and I know what it is to have plenty. I have learned the secret of being content in any and every situation, whether well fed or hungry, whether living in plenty or in want. I can do all this through him who gives me strength" (Philippians 4:11-13 NIV).

This, my friend, is life. And it only comes from Jesus.

All other things that promise life are liars. Their life is counterfeit. Let Jesus' life fill you. You'll be content.

Pursue Christ and really know him as Paul did.

Your Story

- What evidence do you see in your life that you are pursuing Jesus who is the way, the truth and the life?

- Each one of us allows many of the world's offerings of "life" to get in the way of our relationship with Jesus. Which ones are capturing your heart? What are you going to do about it?

The 10 exercises at the end of this book will help you in your battle.

16

Living Freely in Christ

I'm a crazy, lifelong baseball fan. I grew up just three hours from the iconic Baseball Hall of Fame, but strangely, I never went as a kid. However, as an adult, I've been to that remote village of Cooperstown, NY three or four times. Walking through the hallowed room that features the plaques of every hall of famer is an amazing experience. You don't have to be a baseball fan to appreciate the achievements of these men, spanning over 100 years.

One trip to the Hall isn't enough. Every time I go back I'm inspired by that one room, spotlighting baseball's best. Throughout the building, their achievements come to life in ancient videos, play-by-play audio and larger-than-life replicas of some of my childhood heroes.

I keep going back because I'm inspired. I need the shot in the arm, which comes from more than a single glance.

If you need inspiration to live out your faith, turn to Hebrews 11, the spiritual Hall of Fame, or Hall of Faith as many people call it. It's a roster of the great ones, with their achievements spelled out one after another. These men and women are applauded for the way they walked the talk, sometimes in the hardest of circumstances.

Every time I read this landmark chapter, my faith grows. I'm ready to take on the world and live my faith with more conviction. I find strength in reading their stories.

One chapter later, here's the setting described by the writer of Hebrews: "Since we are surrounded by such a great cloud of witnesses…" While I'm looking to the men and women of chapter 11 as my inspiration, I'm even more hyped by knowing that they are surrounding me in the stands, witnessing my walk of faith. Whether they really see me or not, the principle fires me up. We are like the great ones when we faithfully live out our walk with God.

But that's not the secret to living the Christian life. Inspiration doesn't cut it. It just sets the stage.

Look for the answers in the passage:

"Therefore, since we are surrounded by such a great cloud of witnesses, let us throw off everything that hinders and the sin that so easily entangles. And let us run with perseverance the race marked out for us, fixing our eyes on Jesus, the pioneer and perfecter of faith. For the joy set before him he endured the cross, scorning its shame, and sat down at the right hand of the throne of God. Consider him who endured such opposition from sinners, so that you will not grow weary and lose heart" (Hebrews 12:1-3 NIV).

We're called to "throw off everything that hinders" and to cast away "the sin that so easily entangles." Confess and repent. When I think of those faithful ancients, I'm inspired to throw off and cast away. I'll break free from chains and sin.

How?

The most important instruction is found in verse 2: "Fixing our eyes on Jesus." With all encumbrances thrown off and sin repented, looking straight into the eyes and heart of Jesus is the answer to living by faith. The combination of those three elements is incredibly powerful. Let's take a look.

"Throw off anything that hinders." We usually look at sin as the only entanglement in our relationship with God. But there's so much more that can hinder. Outside influences blister our faith. We get caught up in busyness, Netflix, kids' activities, financial pursuits, church commitments, social events and a myriad of other distractions and responsibilities. None of these are wrong, but when they pile up, they hinder our walk of faith. We can't possibly carry the weight of all of them and thrive in our relationship with God. We squeeze him out.

Sometimes, it's good to take an inventory. Prune your life. Throw off anything that hinders. Get back into something manageable. And most importantly, make time for Jesus. Give him your best time. Work everything else around him. If your relationship with Jesus is fading, you know it's time to throw off the hindrances.

What are the hindrances in your life? With wisdom from God, throw some overboard so you have time to freely experience Jesus. Some of these things might be temporary discards, but a few of the hindrances need to be gone forever.

"And the sin that so easily entangles." This needs little explanation. Sin destroys our walk of faith. Our relationship with Jesus is crushed. The solution is to repent and turn back to him. I shared in detail about this in Chapter 10. Once you make the 180-degree turnaround, start fresh and do the third thing the writer states.

"Fixing our eyes on Jesus." This is the heart of the passage. Fixing means to *look away from all else*. Without Christ as the focus of your attention, you'll drift back into hindrances and entanglements. You might default to performance Christianity. Look to Jesus. He loves you, purifies you, draws you to the Father, inspires you, re-centers you and empowers you. Get to know your amazing Savior.

Let me help you with these thought-starters:

Who is he? The writer says he is the pioneer and perfecter of faith. What does that mean? You could spend the next month discovering these qualities of Jesus.

The writer also tells us that joy motivated Jesus to endure the cross. What was that joy? Studying this principle for a few days will help you know the heart of Jesus. ***He brings up the fact that Jesus scorned the shame of the cross.*** That's worth studying further. Scorn is an intense emotion and Jesus felt it. Find out why as you spend time with Jesus and in the Word. ***Jesus sat down at the right hand of the throne of God.*** Imagine graduating from the scornful cross to the greatest place of honor at the Father's right hand. This Jesus, the one you want to know, did just that. What an adventure to study the journey of our Savior. When you fix your eyes on Jesus, you're fixing them on Jesus on the throne, right next to the Father. This is the victorious Jesus.

Can you see the benefits of fixing your eyes on Jesus? The more you understand who he is, the more you'll look differently and intently into his face. Look away from all else. Then you'll know your Savior more intimately as the seasons go by.

This is so practical. Practicing Hebrews 12:1-2 is not meant to be hidden in your quiet time. It's for living. As you press through the day, running up against those things that hinder and entangle, go to Jesus. Cast off the encumbrances. If necessary, confess sin. Then fix your eyes on Jesus, seated on the throne at the right hand of God.

Your Story

Here's the cherry on top of the ice cream sundae of knowing Jesus. The writer of Hebrews explains that knowing Jesus translates into a strong walk of faith. He says that we are to *fix our eyes* on Jesus and *consider* him "so that you will not grow weary and lose heart" (Hebrews 12:3 NIV).

I want that, don't you? Don't you hate it when you're tired and discouraged? The solution is fixing your eyes on Jesus. It's more than just gazing into his eyes. The writer says *consider*. "Consider him who endured..." Think carefully about him.

As I walked through the Hall of Fame looking at the plaques, watching the videos and listening to the play-by-plays from decades ago, I thought about those men who were portrayed. I studied each scene, imagined being there and read the biographies. I went deeper than a quick glance and a bland acknowledgment. I *considered*. And that's what made it so meaningful.

- When you spend time with Jesus, think carefully about him. Unrushed and in a quiet setting, consider him, the author and perfecter of faith. The one who endured. He who is at the right hand of the Father. Get to know him deeply.

Take time now, or in the next 24 hours, to open your Bible to Hebrews 12:1-3. Study these verses. Ask God to open them up to you as you learn to *consider* Jesus.

[For a deeper study of Hebrews, I recommend the *Hebrews Bible Study Guide* from the *Life Change Series* by NavPress].

Tim's Story

Fasting and Filling the Time with Jesus

The subject of intimacy with Jesus has intrigued me all my life. For several years, I've been in persistent prayer for and in pursuit of that intimacy. In my journey, one of the most difficult, but most beneficial, spiritual disciplines I'm developing is fasting.

Throughout my life, I've known a few people who are very intimate with Jesus. Fasting is a practice that has linked each one. While there are other important disciplines, I've found that this one is very rarely spoken of. It's definitely not valued as an essential and reoccurring discipline.

At the core of fasting is *denial of self and dependency on Jesus*. The human body was created to enjoy food and be sustained by its consumption. Consequently, we are to use it in this way. Nonetheless, we see many occasions in Scripture—including in Jesus' life—where the denial of food for spiritual reasons was an expectation.

"When you fast, do not look somber as the hypocrites do, for they disfigure their faces to show others they are fasting. Truly I tell you, they have received their reward in full. But when you fast, put oil on your head and wash your face, so that it will not be obvious to others that you are fasting, but only to your Father, who is unseen; and your Father, who sees what is done in secret, will reward you" (Matthew 6:16-18 NIV).

On this journey, Jesus has given me a phrase that is very difficult to accept. "If you can't say 'No' to food, you can't say 'No' to sin!" This has hit me hard. It's causing me to realize how spiritually weak I am but how spiritually strong Jesus desires for me to be. I'm also understanding the need to increase my level of dependency on Jesus and my intimacy with him.

As a self-proclaimed self-made man, I'm under the illusion that I control the circumstances of my life. While I do believe I have personal responsibility to obey Scripture and to emulate Jesus' life and example, there still lies within me the false belief that "I can do it myself." Thus, my dependency on Jesus takes constant work.

Far too often, I think I can say no to sin in my own power. Without his help. Without being intimate with him. Fasting brings a quick reality check for me.

Practically speaking, I've found that when my physical body craves food, I should fill that time with Jesus. He and he alone can sustain me and give me the strength to say no to food and no to sin.

It all comes back to Jesus and my relationship with him.

Tim Epling is a pastor, encourager and discipler of leaders.

17

Knowing Christ Consistently

As wonderful as it is to experience joy in knowing Christ, you'll fight opposition to this new way of living. How crazy to think that you would trade this abundant life for *garbage*, as Paul calls it. It makes no sense.

However, we do foolish things as Christians. Our sin nature plagues us, the world attracts us and Satan wears us down. Praise God that we have his Holy Spirit to empower us to victory in our relationship with Christ. As we explored in chapter 2, the Holy Spirit miraculously brought our spirit to life when we first came to know Jesus.

When you put this book down, I want you to experience the adventure of knowing Christ consistently. That's what this final chapter is about.

When Performance Pulls Us

How easy it is to default to our old, frustrating way of living the Christian life. Our inner Pharisee pops his head up.

Jesus' illustration of the old and new wineskins is a refreshing wake-up call when we go back to performance Christianity. And that can happen often.

For instance, we love to-do lists. Accomplishing tasks and crossing them off is satisfying. When I was a teen-ager, I pulled out a blank sheet of paper every day and wrote out my schedule. Every hour was spoken for. Every task was documented in advance. I was primed for the day. This way of life is strange for a teen-ager, but I guess I was a strange kid. With a performance-based mentality drilled into me (by myself), it wrecked me when I became a Christian.

When we try the *to-do* method in the Christian life, we're left with emptiness instead of fulfillment. I found that to be true. I was a functioning performaholic for Jesus.

I tried to transfer my to-do list mentality – which worked well in sports, schoolwork and my job – to my walk with God. As I shared in the opening pages, my Christian life dried up. Outward signs were falsely verifying my spiritual growth while I was crumbling inside. I didn't know Jesus intimately. I knew *about* him and what I thought he wanted me to *do*.

We need to take Jesus' illustration to heart:

"Neither is new wine put into old wineskins. If it is, the skins burst and the wine is spilled and the skins are destroyed. But new wine is put into fresh wineskins, and so both are preserved" (Matthew 9:17 ESV).

The old, dried wineskins, when filled with new wine, would burst as the wine fermented. What a mess. Kind of describes our Christian life sometimes.

With the new wineskins, Jesus is referring to the New Covenant he had brought to mankind. This New Covenant would be complete once he died for our sins and was resurrected. The Jews were law-keepers, measuring their spirituality by how well they kept God's commandments and obeyed the Lord's directives. Does that sound familiar? It may describe your life. It certainly all-too-often describes mine.

The old wineskins represent the Old Covenant, keeping the law. The new wineskins represent the New Covenant, living by faith in Christ. He had introduced a way of life that was incomprehensible to the Jews, especially the Pharisees, who had built centuries of law-abiding into their thinking and religion. His new ways didn't fit into their old ways, many of which were not God-given at all.

As theologian Albert Barnes so aptly explained about Jesus' words, "It is not 'fit' that my doctrine should be attached to or connected with the old and corrupt doctrines of the Pharisees. New things should be put together, and made to match." [Barnes' Notes on the Bible--https://biblehub.com/commentaries/matthew/9-17.htm]

When Jesus came, he brought new wineskins. We can live by his doctrine of faith, in relationship with him, instead of relying on obeying the law to achieve relationship with God. In fact, if you pour your Christian life into the old wineskins, the skins will burst. They are destroyed and the wine (your life) is spilled all over the place.

However, pour your spiritual life into the new wineskins (living by faith) and both are preserved.

Knowing Christ is at the center of New Covenant living. We reject the thought that obeying all the commandments in Scripture will make us more spiritual. We embrace living by faith in Christ, knowing and loving him deeply. We live *with* him and thus *for* him. They merge into one, united by the common thread of knowing him.

Obviously, we are to obey God and keep his commandments. Jesus preached on it. And Paul said, "What shall we say, then? Is the law sinful? Certainly not!" (Romans 7:7 NIV). But my point is this: knowing Christ leads to obedience. How empty we are when we attempt flesh-empowered obedience. We are to obey by faith, as did God's obedient pioneers, applauded in Hebrews 11 (NIV):
- *"By faith* Abel brought God a better offering" (v. 4).
- *"By faith* Noah in holy fear built" (v. 7).
- *"By faith* Abraham obeyed" (v. 8).

- *"By faith* Moses refused to be known as the son of Pharaoh's daughter" (v. 24).
- *"By faith* the people passed through the Red Sea" (v. 29).

The battle rages inside us because our old, sinful nature defaults to the law. Not to all of the 613 commands of the Old Testament Torah, but to Christian behaviors.

Our new nature defaults to Christ. It's about our relationship with him before all else.

Whenever you find yourself spiritually dry, empty, frustrated and distant from God, think of Jesus' illustration of the wineskins. Toss out the old – living by the law – and grab the new. Live by faith in him.

You tried unsuccessfully to follow the law in self-effort. Instead, obey Christ out of your deep love for him. It will become a natural result of knowing Jesus.

Remember Paul's words, "What is more, I consider everything a loss because of the surpassing worth of knowing Christ Jesus my Lord" (Philippians 3:8 NIV).

When the World Pushes Us

Pushing back against the ways of the world is exhausting. We're hounded by things opposed to living out our faith. Morality has degenerated, Christian principles have eroded, openness to the gospel is rare. If we stand for our Christian convictions, we're scorned as closed-minded.

Welcome to the days of the early church. These new believers were weird. They practiced humility, love, holiness, sexual faithfulness and a host of other things contrary to their hedonistic environment.

They were mocked, disdained, persecuted and hated. It was so bad that many were killed.

Jesus promised that people would hate the disciples. And it happened as he said. Since that day, committed Christ-followers have been rejected by the world.

In many nations, the persecution of Christians has ramped up.

If you stand for the things of the Lord, you're labeled *intolerant*. Christians are taken to court for standing up for their beliefs.

Paul lived in times of much more intense persecution than we do. He was imprisoned, isolated for his faith. His deep relationship with Christ was his only hope. He had Jesus and that was it. At the core, he wanted to know Christ and to keep knowing him. (Philippians 3:8 and 10).

More than ever, we need to know Christ. Not just intellectually, but with our heart.

The deepest knowing is when our heart connects with Jesus' heart.

Recently, it dawned on me that I had been starting my mornings totally wrong. I'd begin by running through the day ahead. I'd think about what's in store, preparing my mind for my scheduled activities and commitments. I wanted to be mentally and emotionally ready!

How foolish. I should start my day with Jesus. If I really want to know him, then I should know him from the moment I wake up. That's the key. I should fill my mind with thoughts of Christ. Enjoy my relationship with him. Pray, meditate on his character, recite his Word. Immerse myself in him.

The day isn't important compared to the significance of Jesus. He must fill my heart and soul. No way should I let my cares flood in. They shouldn't get first place in my mind at 5:30 am. Jesus should. I need to build habits at the beginning of the day that help me know Christ.

I want to know Christ! That's what Paul said. And that's what I need to do. Beginning from the moment I open my eyes.

Imagine how differently I'll face the day. For years, I had been letting the cares of the day pour into my mind, killing my emotions. I sometimes entered the day depressed, discouraged at the least. I had lost my joy. I wasn't looking forward to the day God had given me. I saw it as a burden and wanted to escape. Day after day, week after week, year after year. I had missed the very thing I had discovered and had been teaching—knowing Christ.

As I know Christ in the morning, my spirit is set for the day.

More than that, my priorities are set. Jesus is right there at the top.

> "I will sing aloud of your steadfast love in the morning" (Psalm 59:16 ESV).
> "In the morning, Lord, you hear my voice; in the morning I lay my requests before you and wait expectantly" (Psalm 5:3 NIV).
> "Let me hear in the morning of your steadfast love" (Psalm 143:8 ESV).
> "I rise before dawn and cry for help; I hope in your words" (Psalm 119:147 ESV).

Going to God first, as soon as I open my eyes, is the solution. Praise God!

Retreating with God

With all the opposition that you'll face, you'll need to fight for your relationship with Jesus. You don't want to go back to the prison of performance Christianity. Because you've lived that way for so long, it will tantalize you until you build the habit of relating to Jesus the right way. The Holy Spirit will change your life. He will also be your greatest helper, guide and advocate as you know Christ the way Paul modeled for us.

The most crucial consistent step you can take is to retreat monthly with God. I've been doing it for years and it has proven to be my lifesaver in my new life of knowing Christ. For me, it's a half day. For others, it's a full day.

It has become a reset for me. All the junk that I deal with accumulates in my heart as the days go by. While I meet with God every morning for a quiet time, there's something life-changing about blocking out a few hours. This reset points me back to true North—Jesus. My heart is cleansed. Burdens are cast off. My mind is cleared. My soul is refreshed. My spirit is renewed. It's nothing short of miraculous.

If you're intrigued by this experience, then I've included a guide to taking a day away with God. It's called ***Retreating with***

Jesus: The Secret to Knowing His Heart, Appendix B to this book. If it sounds like a major undertaking, then the guide is perfect to get you started. As I said, this is life-changing.

Your Story

- What things send you back to performance Christianity?

- Here's an important question to close with: As you've read this book, how is God leading you on the road to overcoming performance Christianity? Think through the key ideas, Scriptures, lessons and principles that have resonated with you. Most of all, pray that the Holy Spirit will reveal those to you.

Closing Thoughts on Our Stories

My Story

I've experienced a breakthrough and I want to bring other believers with me.

This book in your hands is a major stride towards telling so many Christians about the life-changing truth of knowing Christ. Hopefully, your life will be different as you begin the 10 exercises in Appendix A.

Where do I go from here to get the word out? The performer in me wants to develop a strategic plan with a vision, mission and goals. But I won't. I'm leaving that in God's hands. I'm trusting him to do the work. I'm experienced in media and I suspect he'll use my writing, radio and other media skills in the process.

Along with this book, God birthed the **FRESH FAITH 24/7** ministry, the **Overcoming Performance Christianity** podcast and the series of **Your Life With God** devotionals. He has given me multiple opportunities to share this exciting way of life on Christian radio and podcasts.

I will follow Jesus in the journey. I'll be there for you and others who join me. But I won't let this pursuit overshadow my relationship with God. Spending time with Jesus is my treasured oasis. If I get out of line, I'll stop, repent, regroup and then start again.

Thank you for investing the time to read this book. It means a lot to me. Let me know how I can pray for you as you begin this new way of living. My email address is at the end of this chapter.

Your Story

Now that you've read the book, your inner Pharisee has been silenced. You're healed of performance Christianity. Not! It's obvious that what got you into performance prison has deep roots. It will take time to experience true freedom from the bondage of performance Christianity.

As a performer, your solution is to fight against performance. Ironically, that's performance in itself. You rely on your own human effort. How has that worked out so far in your Christian life?

I'm being direct because I want to leave you with a harsh warning and loving counsel that will change your story.

Stop performing for Christ. Know him.

The secret to freedom from the bondage of performance Christianity is not *fighting* it. The secret is moving in the other direction towards Jesus.

Knowing Christ will take time. But the power of the Holy Spirit is there for you. God lives inside you. He loves you. He empowers you. He draws you to himself. Jesus wants to know you.

Early on in this book, I said that your effort to know Christ doesn't define your relationship with him. Your effort helps you *know* him.

From here...

> **Begin the exercises in Appendix A.** Yield to the Holy Spirit and he will reveal Jesus to you in a fresh, deep and intimate way.
>
> **Protect your time with God.** It's basic but so important.
>
> **Share your freedom journey with others.** Do you know other believers who are struggling with performance Christianity? Most often, you don't know until you start talking about it. People will look up when you say that you've silenced your inner Pharisee. You can become an ambassador for a new, extraordinary way of living—free from performance.

Help your Christian friends know the Christ of the cross. Here are a couple practical ideas. First, give them a copy of this book or tell them where they can get a copy. Over the years, I've done that with the three books that have changed my life. And second, send them the link to *FRESH FAITH 24/7*: www.freshfaith247.com.

Finally, I invite you to join the *FRESH FAITH 24/7* ministry. You'll engage with like-minded believers who are on the path to freedom from the bondage of performance Christianity. You'll have 24/7 access to a wealth of benefits and resources that will keep you on the path, starting with the **Freedom Path Training** videos. Find out more at www.freshfaith247.com.

And with that, I will leave you to take advantage of the resources that follow. They will lead you into greater intimacy with our Savior. Please let me know how you're doing as you live the adventure of *knowing Jesus*. It silences your inner Pharisee. Knowing Jesus is the secret to life.

Write me at jon@freshfaith247.com.

How has God used *Silence Your Inner Pharisee* in your life? Leave a favorable Amazon review so others can discover this book, too. Your review makes a difference. Thanks!
amazon.com/dp/B0C6W48CFN

Acknowledgements

I am grateful for a few good friends who were transparent enough to share their stories in this book, bringing to life the biblical principle of knowing Christ: Larry Walters, Jim Van Houten, Lisa Hall, Tim Epling, Parker J. Cole, Ralf Stores and my wife, Noonie.

Thank you to those who reviewed the manuscript before it went to press and provided your kind words of endorsement at the beginning of the book. You invested your time and lent your good names, and I am honored.

Thank you to another handful of people whose opinions I respect. I asked you to read through the rough manuscript to see if this book was worthy to be published. You gave me some good critical insight and God used you to affirm that I should move ahead. You told me the book had wings.

Thank you, Noonie, for cheering me on. I stowed away in my writing room week after week, month after month. You kept asking me, "How's it going?" And I kept saying, "Fine." You even took me out for a congratulations dinner before the book was finished.

Deep thanks to my editor, Pat Clawson. You painstakingly read through every word and sentence—more than once. Then you sat with me by phone for hours at a time, running through every edit and explaining why. We had some deep discussions. You always said the changes were up to me. But as you'll see, almost every one of them was made. I value your professional and theological input, as well as your commitment to excellence in the Lord's work.

You came through once again, Chris Lilly. You've been my cover designer since my first book. This one was a wrestling match for you, as you went through a number of renditions to get it just right. We won't show anyone the concepts that didn't work. Thank you for sticking with it. God used you.

Phil Stacey, thank you for your willingness to write the Foreword. If anyone can relate to performance Christianity, it's you. You know what it is like to battle performance so that your relationship with Christ remains the focus. Your contribution to this book was invaluable.

Thank you, God, for giving me the power through your Holy Spirit to see this project all the way to completion. It has been a multi-year effort. I never lost my drive to see it through. The project always felt fresh. I sensed that the message in the book was one that needed to be communicated. Lord, you affirmed it through the encouraging words of others along the way. And you empowered me to keep going to the end.

Finally, I thank the Apostle Paul. When he wrote these words to the Philippians, he had no idea they would change my life 2,000 years later: ***"What is more, I consider everything a loss because of the surpassing worth of knowing Christ Jesus my Lord, for whose sake I have lost all things. I consider them garbage, that I may gain Christ"*** (Philippians 3:8 NIV). That verse has led to my transformation as I've gone deeper and deeper in knowing Christ. It is the secret to life.

HAVE YOU TAKEN IT YET?

TAKE THE SPIRITUAL SELF-ASSESSMENT

www.freshfaith247.com/assessment

APPENDIX A: Exercises in Knowing Jesus

You've made the time for knowing Jesus. You've found your place to get alone with him. Your heart is ready to seek him.

However, you can quickly go down a winding road with a lot of rabbit trails. Getting lost kills the motivation for knowing Jesus.

Let's see what the Bible has in store that opens up the character and person of Jesus. Knowing about Jesus will help you know him better.

In this section, I've included 10 exercises, or *experiences*, to engage with Jesus, highlighting a different quality or identity of Jesus in each one. Spend a day with each experience. Or spend a week. There are no rules. Read the commentary and answer the questions. Journal if you'd like. The most important thing is that you spend time getting to know Jesus. Before every experience, ask the Holy Spirit to open your heart and reveal something new to you about Jesus.

I encourage you to explore the Bible passage in context. In other words, read the whole chapter. God will show you things outside the short commentary and verses I give you.

Are you ready?

Let's get to know Jesus.

Experience #1: Jesus is the Light of the World

Are you the kind of person who needs it pitch dark in order to sleep? Annoying points of blue light coming from random electronics in the room can drive you crazy. Then there's the alarm clock with the bright red light silently shouting the time at you.

We certainly want it dark to sleep, but most of the time we need light. Driving down a two-lane road at night, I click my headlights on "bright" so I don't miss a turn and plunge into a ditch.

One of the greatest "light" statements in the Bible was announced by Jesus himself:

"I am the light of the world. Whoever follows me will never walk in darkness, but will have the light of life" (John 8:12 NIV).

Jesus doesn't shine the light. He *is* the light. Hang around him and you'll have enough insight and clarity to take the next step, no matter what you're facing.

Are you struggling with raising your kids? (It's normal!) Jesus is the light. He'll give you insight to deal wisely with the issues you're facing.

Are you facing a major decision? Jesus is the light. He'll grant you wisdom.

Are you discouraged? Jesus is the light. He'll walk you through the dark jungle that has you down.

Are you tempted by a certain sin? Jesus is the light. Invite him into your battle. His holiness will expose the ugliness of your sin. His power will help you overcome.

Notice that Jesus says, ". . . whoever follows me." Let Jesus lead you, just like you'd have a guide lead you on a Himalayan hike. Stay close behind Jesus for the journey. Hold onto his robe if you need to. Some journeys are more dangerous than others.

No matter what, follow Jesus as if your life depended on it. It does. Follow desperately. It's when you decide that you don't need the Light of the World that you'll stumble and fall.

Jesus promises that you'll have the light of *life* when you follow him. Indeed, he is talking about eternal life, but you'll also experience life here on earth. A wholeness and fullness that only comes from a right relationship with God.

Jesus lights the way to the Father. He also gives you light today to live for him. Welcome the Light of the World into your day. Seek his face and he will light the way.

READ:

John 8:12

REFLECT:

1. Think of a time when darkness confused or disoriented you. What happened when you turned on the light?

2. Where do you need the Light of the World today?

3. When you have the light of life, how will that make a difference in an area of darkness you are facing?

PRAY:

Pray that Jesus will lead you out of any darkness you are experiencing (sin, toxic relationships, spiritual oppression) and lead you into his light. In his light, you will experience freedom in your walk with Christ. When you find these dark things creep back into your life, go again to the Light of the world, Jesus.

Experience #2: Jesus, The True Vine

One of my favorite passages in all of Scripture is John 15:1-8, which holds the secret to living the Christian life. It's a simple concept that I return to often. These verses are a great reminder of how Jesus intended for us to relate to him.

The passage starts out, "I am the true vine" (John 15:1 ESV). I find these words assuring. Jesus' statement sets the scene. He shows me the source of life. He's not just any vine. He's the *true* vine.

Picture a garden with vines running through. You can trace each one to the source of its nutrients. In his analogy, Jesus is likely illustrating with a grape vine, familiar to everyone in that day. Imagine a complex set of intertwined vines crawling up a pole or a fence. We used to have grape vines that continually grew and expanded their reach every year.

This is the picture in John 15. Jesus is the source of life. All other vines find their nutrients in this one true vine. Every shoot that emerges from Jesus the true vine should be full of life.

But that doesn't always happen. Some branches die. They've stopped absorbing their nutrients from the true vine.

Jesus says it this way about our relationship with him, "Whoever abides in me, and I in him, he it is that bears much fruit, for apart from me you can do nothing" (John 15:5 ESV).

It's so simple! All we need to do is abide. That's an ancient word that needs some clarification. It means to remain in, dwell in, live in.

It's more than *connecting to*, because dead branches are still connected to the vine. You can have a relationship with Jesus, but as they say, you could be "dying on the vine." You might describe your Christian life as lackluster, boring, dry or stale.

I think the best phrase to make it clear is "live in." Am I living in Christ? In an instant, I bet you can answer that question. You know whether you are *living in* Christ or not.

What could be blocking spiritual nutrients coming to you from Jesus the true vine?

You may not be spending time getting to know Jesus, enjoying his presence by talking to him (praying) and reading the Bible. A half hour each day, away from noise and distractions, can make a big difference.

Perhaps sin is junking up the pathway from Christ to you. Impurities will block nutrients from the vine to the branch and kill it off.

Or maybe you're trying too hard to live the Christian life. Look again at John 15:5 and see what Jesus says about bearing fruit: "Whoever abides in me, and I in him, he it is that bears much fruit." A branch doesn't exert any effort to produce fruit. It simply absorbs nutrients from the trunk or vine and the grapes appear.

Turning away from Christ to produce fruit on our own is not only futile, it's an insult to Jesus.

Live in Christ, the true vine.

READ:

Read John 15:1-8

"I am the true vine, and my Father is the vinedresser. Every branch in me that does not bear fruit he takes away, and every branch that does bear fruit he prunes, that it may bear more fruit. Already you are clean because of the word that I have spoken to you. Abide in me, and I in you. As the branch cannot bear fruit by itself, unless it abides in the vine, neither can you, unless you abide in me. I am the vine; you are the branches. Whoever abides in me and I in him, he it is that bears much fruit, for apart from me you can do nothing. If anyone does not abide in me he is thrown away like a branch and withers; and the branches are gathered, thrown into the fire, and burned. If you abide in me, and my words abide in you, ask whatever you wish, and it will be done for you. By this my Father is glorified, that you bear much fruit and so prove to be my disciples" (ESV).

REFLECT:

1. Journal your thoughts about this passage. What jumps out at you?

2. What do these words and phrases mean to you?

    "I am the true vine" (Jesus) _____

    abide _____

    fruit _____

3. Who is Jesus according to this passage? Describe him.

4. What quality of God do you want to get to know better?

PRAY:

Read John 15:1-8 aloud. Then pray about becoming an *abiding believer*.

Experience #3: Jesus, the Alpha and the Omega

"I am the Alpha and the Omega, the First and the Last, the Beginning and the End" (Revelation 22:13 NIV).
What do those words do for you when you read them? For me, they give me a sense of awe. I feel energized. I want to praise Jesus!
"Long live the king!" is the shout we hear for human royalty. I want to shout that for Jesus, The King with a capital K.
Jesus is our all in all. Three times in this verse he announces his eternal existence. What a mind-blowing thought. Jesus *from* all eternity *into* all eternity.
Can you wrap your mind around the eternal existence of Jesus? If you can't, that's ok. We shouldn't be able to understand it fully with our limited, human minds. The thought of the eternal Jesus is beyond us.
How is it possible to have an intimate relationship with Jesus, who is the Beginning and the End? The contrast of the infinitely huge to the infinitely personal is extraordinary. The beauty is that while Jesus is eternal, he also longs to have a deep relationship with you.
The Apostle John felt the same awe that you feel. Even after spending three years with him! While in exile many years later, he wrote in Revelation, "When I saw him, I fell at his feet as though dead. Then he placed his right hand on me and said: 'Do not be afraid. I am the First and the Last'" (Revelation 1:17 NIV).
It's as if Jesus sets aside certain character qualities that would make us shudder in awe. And then he sits with us as our personal, loving Savior. We need both. We need to know he is the Alpha and the Omega while we experience his cross-bearing love for us.
Jesus is your all in all, the eternal God who came to earth to have a personal relationship with humanity. With you.

READ:

Consider Revelation 1:17-18 (NIV). Alone in exile in the latter days of his life, the apostle John wrote these words about Jesus:

"When I saw him, I fell at his feet as though dead. Then he placed his right hand on me and said: 'Do not be afraid. I am the First and the Last. I am the Living One; I was dead, and now look, I am alive for ever and ever!'"

Read these words, also written by John, during his season of ministry -- I John 3:1-2 (NIV):

"See what great love the Father has lavished on us, that we should be called children of God! And that is what we are! The reason the world does not know us is that it did not know him. Dear friends, now we are children of God, and what we will be has not yet been made known. But we know that when Christ appears, we shall be like him, for we shall see him as he is."

REFLECT:

1. As you consider Jesus right now, complete these sentences:

    - When I think of Jesus as the Alpha and the Omega, the First and the Last, I ...

    - When I think of Jesus as my personal Savior, and consider the Father as *my* Father, I ...

2. Ponder the answers you gave. Add more thoughts. Let your mind run free.

3. You are a child of the God of the universe. He is your Father. Think about that. What are the benefits of being his child? How does it make you feel?

4. What quality of God do you want to get to know better?

PRAY:

Do you need to trust Jesus with something that burdens you? Something that is constantly on your mind? Spend time praying to your loving Savior about this, claiming his promise, "Come to me, all you who are weary and burdened, and I will give you rest" (Matthew 11:28 NIV). Be honest with Jesus. Spend as much time as you need. Other burdens might come to mind, too. Talk with Jesus and release your burdens to him.

Take time to thank your loving heavenly Father that you are in his family. All because of his Son's death on the cross. Give the Father thanks for the benefits you reflected on earlier.

Experience #4: Jesus My Shepherd

Did you know that shepherds give names to their sheep? And that when they call their sheep, the sheep answer to their name? Jesus was telling it like it is in John 10:3, "He calls his own sheep by name and leads them out" (NIV).

I'm so glad I have the greatest shepherd in the world taking care of me. Jesus. Here's what I know about Jesus, my shepherd, in his own words:

I am the good shepherd. Jesus is all in with me. Unlike the hired hand, contract labor, Jesus is here to protect me at all costs. "The good shepherd lays down his life for the sheep," says Jesus in verse 11. He proved it on the cross and he proves it today. Jesus protects me from the enemy, Satan, who is out to devour me like wolves devour sheep.

Second, Jesus says, **I know my sheep.** What an incredible truth. The Son of God, Lord of all, isn't too busy running the universe to know me personally. I'm special to him. So special that he not only knows my name, but knows my heart, mind, emotions and personality. He knows my ways. Then he says, "My sheep know me." This knowing is a two-way street. Jesus and I have a close personal relationship.

And third, Jesus says, **"I am the gate for the sheep."** The gate was the way in and out for the sheep, but it was also the protective door to ward off wolves and robbers. The shepherd would lay down at the opening of the pen and be a human gate. Jesus is that gate for us. The one who lays down his life.

While the good shepherd knows us and protects us, he also leads us into life. "I have come that they may have life, and have it to the full" (John 10:10 NIV). He did it the moment we came to salvation. And he continues today, leading us into life, protection, fullness, love, care and so much more in his safety.

The good shepherd also provides something more. Other sheep! Sheep hang out together. We need to be with other believers to fully experience the blessings and protection of the good shepherd. That's why a solid church is so important. There's strength when we're there for each other, experiencing worship, teaching, fellowship and encouragement. Sheep don't graze alone, and neither should we.

Why?

We're hassled every day by enemies who would lure us away from the care of Jesus. Temptations entice us to stray from the shepherd. False teachers twist the Word of God, changing it up just enough to make us curious to follow. Certain friends subtly turn our eyes away from our shepherd. Enemies of the cross outright attack our faith on social media to distract us, causing us to retaliate.

What pulls *you* away from the good shepherd, leaving you in danger, isolated and vulnerable?

Choose to put your life in the care of Jesus, the good shepherd. Look to him for physical, spiritual and emotional protection and provision. And join with other believers who are doing the same thing.

READ:

Read John 10:1-17.

REFLECT:

From that passage, notice the qualities of the good shepherd. Write them down or make a mental note of them.

Where are you vulnerable right now and need the protection of the good shepherd?

PRAY:

Come to the good shepherd and share your heart with him. Do you feel safe in his care, right now? Tell him. Are you feeling isolated? Tell him. Are you being attacked by temptation, friends, false teaching or social media attacks on your faith? Tell him. Talk to him about it. Whatever is on your mind right now, share it with the good shepherd. Trust him with your life.

Experience #5: Jesus My Brother

Have you ever thought of Jesus as your brother? Lord? *Yes.* Savior? *Yes.* But brother? *Yes again!*

It's often hard to comprehend that the Lord Jesus Christ is also your brother. How can it be?

Think about James, Jesus' brother in the flesh. He was perplexed, too. Jesus was his brother but, after the resurrection, he also regarded Jesus as his Lord. He was a devoted early church follower of his own brother.

Notice Jesus' statement in Mark 3:34-35 (ESV): "He looked at those seated in a circle around him and said, 'Here are my mother and my brothers! Whoever does God's will is my brother and sister and mother.'"

When you were adopted into God's family through salvation, you immediately became a brother of Jesus. Although you're considered a brother by adoption, Jesus doesn't see it that way. He sees you as his full-fledged brother. This spiritual relationship is far more important to Jesus than the physical relationships of family.

Consider this promise: "For he who sanctifies and those who are sanctified all have one source. That is why he is not ashamed to call them brothers" (Hebrews 2:11 ESV).

Jesus calls you his brother.

When I think about this, it melts my heart. It doesn't change the fact that I worship my Lord and Savior. However, there are times that I need a brother to pour my heart out to. I need someone, like my brother Bob, that I can bounce off ideas, share my struggles, ask advice and just spend time with.

Jesus is the best brother you or I can ever have. He's the perfect brother. Is your mind spinning as you think about this? The Lord of the universe has come down to relate to you as your brother. He lowered himself to assume that role. Because he loves you.

Treasure your relationship with Jesus as your brother. Enjoy it! Enjoy *him*.

What is it that you value in a relationship with a brother? Make a mental or written note right now. Then, throughout the next few days, speak to Jesus as your brother. He wants to hang out with you. Through thick and thin, Jesus your brother is by your side.

READ:

Read Mark 3:31-35 (NIV) and see the full context of Jesus' statement of how he is your brother.

> "Then Jesus' mother and brothers arrived. Standing outside, they sent someone in to call him. A crowd was sitting around him, and they told him, 'Your mother and brothers are outside looking for you.'
>
> "'Who are my mother and my brothers?'" he asked.
>
> "Then he looked at those seated in a circle around him and said, 'Here are my mother and my brothers! Whoever does God's will is my brother and sister and mother.'"

Then let's look at Hebrews 2:11 (ESV) again and God's promise:

> "For he who sanctifies and those who are sanctified all have one source. That is why he is not ashamed to call them brothers."

You are sanctified by Christ. And he is your brother.

REFLECT:

How do you feel, knowing that the Savior of the world, Jesus, is your brother?

Since he is your brother, how should that change or affirm the way you view your relationship with him?

PRAY:

Take time to thank Jesus that you are in his family. All because of his death on the cross.

Spend a few minutes talking to Jesus as your brother. Open your heart to him and share the kinds of things you would share with a close brother.

Experience #6: Jesus My Friend

Several summers ago, our kids hosted a good-bye reception for us before we left Colorado for North Carolina. Spending more than seven years in the Rocky Mountain State, we had developed many good friendships.

I was feeling down with the thought of *celebrating* our departure. I just wanted to slip away rather than go through the pain of saying good-bye to many people we had done life with all those years.

It was also the last day with my brother and his family, who lived just an hour away. We'd be giving up family get-togethers with them. Even more painful would be leaving our son and family, who hosted the open house. We had lived in the same town for three years, developing a strong bond.

Saying good-bye isn't easy.

If you've moved away at some point, you know what I mean. I was sad to leave family and friends.

Then I remembered Jesus. He's a great friend. He would be going to North Carolina with us, just as he had done in our move from California to Colorado several years earlier.

Jesus told his followers, "No longer do I call you servants, for the servant does not know what his master is doing; but I have called you friends" (John 15:15 ESV).

When I think of Jesus as my friend, a warmth soothes my soul. Maybe it's because I picture this King of Kings and Lord of Lords stepping down off his throne and sitting beside me. Friends sit next to each other or across from each other and this is what Jesus does with us.

The great hymn, **What a Friend We Have in Jesus**, goes through my mind:
> "What a friend we have in Jesus,
> All our sins and griefs to bear!
> What a privilege to carry
> Ev'rything to God in prayer!
> Oh, what peace we often forfeit;
> Oh, what needless pain we bear

All because we do not carry
Ev'rything to God in prayer!"

Jesus is a friend who has done much more for you than any other friend you have ever had. He has borne your sins, grief, anxiety, pain — everything that weighs on your heart!

"Greater love has no one than this, that someone lay down his life for his friends" (John 15:13 ESV).

Jesus is a friend who has given his life for you. He continues to be there to bond with you as you do life together. He'll celebrate your victories and put his arm around you in your losses.

I'm not sure if you're going through separation, loneliness, betrayal, grief, anxiety, suffering or some other pain right now. I do know that Jesus is your friend. He sits beside you. He is your faithful friend who gave his life for you and continues to give and give and give.

If you feel like you need a friend these days, you've got one. Jesus. Thank him for his friendship.

READ:

Jesus spoke these words to his disciples, "You are my friends if you do what I command. I no longer call you servants, because a servant does not know his master's business. Instead, I have called you friends, for everything that I learned from my Father I have made known to you" (John 15:14-15 NIV).

As a Christ-follower, you are a friend of Jesus. You're an insider. Jesus is transparent with you, just as you are with your close friends. However, the difference here is that the Son of God is the one who is your friend.

REFLECT:

Why does Jesus connect our obedience to friendship with him?

Have you been a good friend to Jesus this week? If so, how? How can you be a better friend?

How has Jesus shown his friendship to you?

PRAY:

Take a few moments and thank Jesus for his friendship. Then tell him one or two things you'd like him to know about you, your life, a struggle or victory. Just like you would your best friend. He is your best friend. Have a conversation with him.

Or…

Are you experiencing pain right now? Come to Jesus, your friend, and release this pain to him in prayer. Remember the hymn:

> Oh, what peace we often forfeit;
> Oh, what needless pain we bear
> All because we do not carry
> Ev'rything to God in prayer!

Experience #7: Jesus My Lord

When you approach Jesus as Lord, what goes through your mind? For me, I settle into a spirit of stability and rest. The word "Lord" gives me perspective. Jesus is in control. Everyone and everything report to him. I feel stronger after addressing Jesus as Lord. It's like hitting "reset" in my mind and spirit.

"Therefore God exalted Him to the highest place, and gave Him the name above all names, that at the name of Jesus every knee should bow, in heaven and on earth and under the earth, and every tongue confess that Jesus Christ is Lord, to the glory of God the Father" (Philippians 2:9-11 NIV).

We probably address Jesus more as "Lord" than with any other title. We often begin our prayers, "Lord Jesus . . ."

Jesus said to Thomas, "Reach out your hand and put it into my side. Stop doubting and believe." Thomas' immediate response was to call Jesus "Lord." He said, "My Lord and my God!" (John 20:27-28 NIV).

The word "Lord" in the Greek is "kurios" and means master or owner, one who is to be obeyed and who has dominion. In the case of Jesus, his dominion is over the universe. All creation.

We are taught that Jesus is our Lord, and rightly so. As the ruler of the universe, he is also the ruler of our lives. Praise God that Jesus is not a dictator, but a loving Lord who gave his life for us.

I'm humbled when I pray, "Lord Jesus." I recognize him as my master. He has authority over me and I need to submit to him. Willingly. How can I not bow down to a loving Lord who sacrificed his life for me and provides for me every day? Lord Jesus is in charge of heaven and earth. Yes, I am humbled when I address him as Lord.

How does honoring Jesus as Lord affect the way I live? When I pray, "Lord Jesus," the thought of obedience should come to mind. I should feel a sense of responsibility to live the life Jesus desires and not to act like my own master.

When you pray today, begin by saying "Lord Jesus." And then say nothing else. Let those words sink in. Meditate on them. Be quiet before the Lord Jesus. Think through what his title means to you. Be absorbed by the thought of Jesus as Lord.

READ:

Philippians 2:9-11 expresses so well the Lordship of Christ. Read it slowly several times, emphasizing different words as you read.

"Therefore God exalted Him to the highest place, and gave Him the name above all names, that at the name of Jesus every knee should bow, in heaven and on earth and under the earth, and every tongue confess that Jesus Christ is Lord, to the glory of God the Father" (Philippians 2:9-11 NIV).

REFLECT:

When you consider Jesus is Lord of the universe, how does that make you feel?

PRAY:

When you pray today, begin by saying "Lord Jesus." And then say nothing else. Let those words sink in. Meditate on them. Be quiet before the Lord Jesus. Think through what his title means to you. Be absorbed by the thought of Jesus as Lord.

Experience #8: Jesus the Lamb of God

The first identity of Jesus that was declared to the world was spoken by John the Baptist:
"Behold, the Lamb of God, who takes away the sin of the world!" (John 1:29 ESV).

What an entrance! In one sentence, John described Jesus' mission. He came to take away the sin of the world by being slaughtered as a sacrificial lamb.

Word must not have spread far from that spot. For the rest of Jesus' life, his followers thought he was the king that would overthrow Rome.

Even Jesus' disciples never got this Lamb of God thing – until his resurrection. When Jesus explained his torturous future to the 12, Peter would have nothing of it. "Never, Lord!" he said. "This shall never happen to you!" (Matthew 16:22 NIV).

I would not want to play the lamb role in Jesus' day. Every Passover, lambs across Israel were slain as atonement for the sins of the people. Not just any lambs, but the best lambs of all. Unblemished. Spotless. No acne.

What did dying lambs have to do with forgiveness of sin? The writer of Hebrews states plainly, "Without the shedding of blood there is no forgiveness" (Hebrews 9:22 NIV). He is referring to the truth laid out in Leviticus 7:11: "For the life of a creature is in the blood, and I have given it to you to make atonement for yourselves on the altar; it is the blood that makes atonement for one's life" (NIV).

Throughout Jewish history, God commanded blood sacrifice for the forgiveness of sin. That's what makes Jesus' sacrifice so raw.

Jesus was the most perfect Lamb. The song "O Little Town of Bethlehem" focuses on the baby Jesus. However, this little town was the breeding ground for the sacrificial lambs throughout Jewish history.

Lambs were raised here and then brought to Jerusalem for Passover sacrifices. Certainly, lambs were raised in other fields, but only the Bethlehem lambs were considered worthy of giving their lives at Passover. They were the "perfect" lambs.

It is no coincidence that Jesus was born in Bethlehem and died in Jerusalem. No lamb ever raised in Bethlehem was really perfect. Only Jesus was. His sacrifice was counted for the rest of history.

Jesus was the final Lamb. His sacrifice didn't have a one-year expiration date, renewable every Passover. He died for us once and for all.

"Nor did he enter heaven to offer himself again and again, the way the high priest enters the Most Holy Place every year with blood that is not his own. Otherwise Christ would have had to suffer many times since the creation of the world. But he has appeared once for all at the culmination of the ages to do away with sin by the sacrifice of himself" (Hebrews 9:25-26 NIV).

Centuries before John's declaration, Isaiah prophesied about the Messiah of the future. "He was oppressed and afflicted, yet he did not open his mouth; he was led like a lamb to the slaughter, and as a sheep before its shearers is silent, so he did not open his mouth" (Isaiah 53:7 NIV).

I think about all of Jesus' identities that he showed us during his life. Teacher, prophet, light of the world, king and many more that we are exploring in this book. However, none was as important as this one. Had he not been sacrificed as the Lamb of God, we would not have salvation. Satan would not be defeated. All Jesus' teachings would have been nice, but they wouldn't save us.

The central identity of Jesus is the Lamb of God. His central mission was to take away the sin of the world. Note that he was the only lamb in history to *willingly* sacrifice himself, even carrying the wood that was the altar where he was placed.

And he did.

Jesus was the transformed Lamb. Once he was sacrificed and went back to the right hand of the Father, he was the *ruler* Lamb. In Revelation, Jesus is referred to as the Lamb 27 times. No longer the bleeding Lamb on the cross, but the victorious Lamb.

This Lamb was the only one worthy of opening the scroll, the revelation of God's judgment on earth in the last days.

"Then I saw a Lamb, looking as if it had been slain, standing at the center of the throne, encircled by the four living creatures and the elders. He went and took the scroll from the right hand of him who sat on the throne. And when he had taken it, the four living creatures and the twenty-four elders fell down before the Lamb" (Revelation 5:6-8 NIV).

Later in the chapter, tens of thousands of angels affirmed the glory of Jesus the Lamb of God:

"Worthy is the Lamb, who was slain, to receive power and wealth and wisdom and strength and honor and glory and praise!" (verse 12).

It gets better. Every creature on earth joined the chorus of praise:

"To him who sits on the throne and to the Lamb be praise and honor and glory and power, for ever and ever!" (verse 13).

What a contrast between the Lamb in his glory and the sacrificial Lamb on the cross. Jesus is both.

This Lamb possessed the Book of Life.

READ:

Read John 1:29 followed by Revelation 5:6-8

REFLECT:

Contrast Jesus the Lamb in these two passages. Make a list of the qualities of Jesus the Lamb in the first passage and Jesus the Lamb in the second. What differences do you see?

PRAY:

Close your eyes and picture yourself standing alongside one of the 24 elders falling down before the Lamb (Revelation 5:8). Think back on that Scripture. Spend time praising the Lamb and lifting your prayers to him.

Experience #9: Jesus the Living Water

He confused her to no end. Jesus tried to explain to the woman at the well that he was the water she came for. He began by referring to the "living water." That strange concept got her attention.

Thinking on the physical plane, she asked, "Where can you get this living water?"

Now Jesus had her attention. He took a sharp right turn and opened her spiritual eyes. "Everyone who drinks this water will be thirsty again, but whoever drinks the water I give them will never thirst. Indeed, the water I give them will become in them a spring of water welling up to eternal life."

By the end of the conversation, the Holy Spirit had fully enlightened this Samaritan woman. She was so convinced of Jesus' Messiahship that she became a radical evangelist. The story ends with this thrilling statement: "Many of the Samaritans from that town believed in him because of the woman's testimony."

What is this living water? It's a *who*. It's Jesus, of course, our solution for salvation. Jesus' spiritual life-giving water is miraculous. He said, "Whoever believes in me, as Scripture has said, rivers of living water will flow from within them" (John 7:38 NIV). Our salvation is once and for all because of this single drink of the living water.

But there's more. A bonus! John tips us off to the meaning behind Jesus' promise of the *rivers* of living water. "By this he meant the Spirit, whom those who believed in him were later to receive. Up to that time the Spirit had not been given, since Jesus had not yet been glorified" (verse 39).

How blessed we are to have the Holy Spirit as the living water bonus. Do you realize the benefits you possess?

Jesus calls the Holy Spirit our "Advocate" (John 14:26). That word means "helper," coming from the Greek word "paraclete." In that verse, Jesus explains the primary role of the Advocate, saying he "will teach you all things and will remind you of everything I have said to you."

Jesus calls the Holy Spirit "the Spirit of truth" who will "guide you into all the truth" (John 16:13). I need that. I get sidetracked.

The Holy Spirit gives us power. I often do things in my own power. How sad, because God has offered *his* power to do his will.

Jesus promised his disciples, "But you will receive power when the Holy Spirit comes on you; and you will be my witnesses in Jerusalem, and in all Judea and Samaria, and to the ends of the earth" (Acts 1:8 NIV).

We're called to serve Christ, but not in our own power. We possess the explosive and sustaining power of God. Let's draw on the Holy Spirit.

The Holy Spirit reveals the thoughts of God. "The Spirit searches all things, even the deep things of God. For who knows a person's thoughts except their own spirit within them? In the same way no one knows the thoughts of God except the Spirit of God" (1 Corinthians 2:11-12 NIV).

Don't you hate it when your internet goes down? You're cut off from the world.

The Holy Spirit is our "internet connection" to the thoughts of God. He never goes down. You could say we have a direct, broadband connection to the mind of the Lord. We're tuned in to the thoughts of God as a benefit of possessing the Holy Spirit.

If you want to know what God thinks, read the Bible. That's the mind of God that the Holy Spirit will reveal to you. Words on the pages will come alive when the Holy Spirit enlightens you. It's a supernatural experience.

The Holy Spirit prays when we don't know what to pray. "Likewise the Spirit helps us in our weakness. For we do not know what to pray for as we ought, but the Spirit himself intercedes for us with groanings too deep for words" (Romans 8:26 ESV).

There are times when we're speechless before God. Whether we're shocked, confused, distraught or overwhelmed, we just don't know how to pray or what to pray. One of God's greatest promises to the Christian is the Holy Spirit will pray when we can't.

Jesus is the Living Water and the Father sent us the Holy Spirit so rivers of living water would flow into and through us.

READ:

Read John 7:37-38: "On the last and greatest day of the festival, Jesus stood and said in a loud voice, 'Let anyone who is thirsty come to me and drink. Whoever believes in me, as Scripture has said, rivers of living water will flow from within them.' By this he meant the Spirit, whom those who believed in him were later to receive. Up to that time the Spirit had not been given, since Jesus had not yet been glorified" (NIV).

REFLECT:

Of the five qualities of the Holy Spirit discussed above (and there are many more), which ones stand out most to you? Why?

Meditate on this phrase from Jesus: "Rivers of living water will flow from within them." Reflect on this phrase for a couple minutes. How does it make you feel to know that Jesus is talking about you when he says, "them"?

PRAY:

Take time to thank God for these specific Living Water promises of the Holy Spirit:

1. The Holy Spirit your Advocate.
2. The Holy Spirit will guide you into all the truth.
3. The Holy Spirit gives you power.
4. The Holy Spirit reveals the thoughts of God.
5. The Holy Spirit prays when you don't know what to pray.

Finish by talking to God about any issues in your life where you need one or more of these promises of the Holy Spirit.

Experience #10: Jesus the Healer

Doctors treat. God heals.

That's been a motto of mine for a few years. As medicine advances, we put more and more hope in our healthcare system. I'm glad I live today and not 100 years ago.

In Jesus' day, common illnesses often caused death. Today we take a pill for some of those maladies.

As much as we want to put our hope in the medical professionals, medicines and treatments, we need to look to the one who really does the healing. Jesus. He understands the intricacies of our body and the exact nature of our ailments. Every cell is known by him, whether it's healthy or diseased.

Of Jesus' 37 recorded miracles (and these were just a sampling), most of them were healings—Peter's mother-in-law, the leper, the man with the withered hand and the multiple blind men given sight. These are just a few. And let's not forget the breathtaking miracle of raising Lazarus from the dead.

Jesus healed people with little or no faith and those who had great faith. He healed by touch and he healed at a distance. He healed with words and he healed with his hands. There was no pattern for Jesus' healing work. He was Lord and he chose his method of healing.

The one constant is this. Whenever Jesus healed, God was glorified.

One of Jesus' first miracles was a healing he performed in unique fashion. A government official begged Jesus to heal his sick son. Amazing, isn't it, since Jesus had just started his public ministry? We pick up the story in John 4:49.

"The royal official said, 'Sir, come down before my child dies.'

"'Go,' Jesus replied, 'your son will live.'

"The man took Jesus at his word and departed. While he was still on the way, his servants met him with the news that his boy was living. When he inquired as to the time when his son got better, they said to him, 'Yesterday, at one in the afternoon, the fever left him.'

"Then the father realized that this was the exact time at which Jesus had said to him, 'Your son will live.' So he and his whole household believed" (John 4:49-53 NIV).

Jesus healed. But he didn't heal everyone. Men, women and children died every day without the healing touch of Jesus. The omniscient Savior knew about each one, but chose only to heal a few.

The same is true today.

A good friend lost his wife to cancer a few years ago. I remember it like it was yesterday. I was with him in the waiting room at the hospital when the doctor told him that there was nothing more the medical team could do. The doctor recommended hospice. This dear woman of God would be passing away in weeks.

Still, this faithful, godly family kept praying for miraculous healing. They believed, almost to the final day, that she would be healed. But it wasn't so.

Healing is a mystery. We can't begin to understand it. But we do know that Jesus heals. And God wants us to pray for healing, just as we pray for anything else on our heart.

Let's look at Jesus the healer.

He cares. He is so much in love with you that he went to the cross so you could live forever. He abandoned his perfection to take on your sin. That's what I call "caring sacrifice."

He feels. Jesus never had cancer or any other disease. But, if anyone knows what pain and suffering feels like, it's him. Every Easter, we're reminded in vivid detail of his journey to the cross and his painful hours hanging there. He has felt pain and understands yours.

He is with you. A verse that speaks to our emotional pain in the midst of our physical pain is Psalm 34:18 (ESV): "The LORD is near to the brokenhearted and saves the crushed in spirit."

Whether Jesus chooses to heal you quickly, slowly or not at all, it doesn't change *who* he is. He is Jesus the healer, as we see over and over again in the New Testament. And isn't the final healing the most glorious of all? It's the complete healing—100% certain.

Revelation 21:4 (ESV) gives us a hint: "He will wipe away every tear from their eyes, and death shall be no more, neither shall there be mourning, nor crying, nor pain anymore, for the former things have passed away."

Praise Jesus the healer.

READ:

Read John 4:43-53, the complete exciting story of the government official's son.

REFLECT:

What stands out about this healing?

How does this passage encourage you?

Who do you know that needs healing?

Think about what God is teaching you about Jesus the healer.

PRAY:

Pray for people in your life who need healing. One of those may be you. Write their names down and commit them into the Lord's care. While we don't understand why God heals some, and not others, we are told to pray for them.

APPENDIX B:
Retreating with Jesus – The Secret to Knowing His Heart

David made a remarkable statement in one of the Psalms:
"The words of the Lord are pure words,
like silver refined in a furnace on the ground,
purified seven times" (Psalm 12:6 ESV).
There are times when I've needed to hear that. The words of God stand out in their purity. David goes to the extreme when he said God's words are like silver purified seven times. He chose "seven" because it is the perfect number throughout biblical history. When I let the words of the Lord penetrate my soul, they purify me. Perfectly.

Some days, I need that purity. I focus so much on output that my well runs dry. And what better way to fill the well of my soul than with the perfect, 100% pure words of God?

I remember a day when after reading that Psalm and one more, I dove into Revelation. I was studying it in depth that season. I read, meditated, wrote out my thoughts and scribbled the answer to one revealing question from the study guide I was using. God refreshed me with his Word. It purified me. I felt my well filling up.

Knowing Jesus is much the same way. We can't constantly serve him unless we are consistently filled up by *knowing* him. Knowing Jesus is input. Serving him is output.

Just as the words of God are perfectly pure, Jesus is, too. And we need time in his presence for our relationship to be fed.

Without time alone with Jesus, we'll fade back into the "service first" mentality that pushes us back into performance Christianity.

Our time with Jesus isn't a ritual. It's a necessity. It develops the love relationship.

Where do you stand in your input/output balance? Is it time to carve out an extended time to retreat with God?

One of the richest spiritual experiences I enjoy is taking a day away with God. I've heard others say the same thing. My daily quiet times are a lifeline, but this monthly retreat is life-*changing*. I can't believe I waited so many years to start! I encourage you to start as soon as possible.

Here are a few of my insights:

1. There's something special that happens when I have unrushed, often unstructured, time with God. I push away my regular activities and responsibilities to be with Jesus. It's that simple. Yet, profound at the same time.
2. While I experience tremendous benefits from my day away with God, it's not really about me. The day with Him is a time of fellowship and communion at a level that can't happen any other way. My day away with God is really about Him. And I receive so many benefits.
3. Sometimes I start by praying. Other times I begin by camping on a passage from Scripture. Or I might turn up praise music to get started. There are times I have more structure to my day. But I have one rule . . . there are *no* rules!

If, at this moment, you're thinking, "I need this!" then that's God drawing you to himself. He desires the time with you. He loves you.

However, it may be impossible to carve out a full day to be with Jesus.

Your life may revolve around young children or even a new baby in the home. Your job may be so demanding you can't take time off any time soon. You might even be working two jobs and barely have enough time to eat and sleep. You're exhausted! Or it could be that you and God aren't getting along that well right now.

If any of those situations describes your life, then you need a retreat with God more than ever. Obstacles like this are Satan's way of keeping you from God. You'll end up spiraling down further and further emotionally, physically and spiritually.

Whether you're life is crazy or things are good and steady, you need a Sabbath rest. A retreat with God is a time of restoration.

The most important thing you can do at this moment is to say, "Yes, I will carve out time to get away with God to restore my soul."

Making It Happen

To put you at ease, let me say that there is nothing magical about a full day. If you can only set aside a half day, do it! If you have to get up in the middle of the night and begin at 3 am before work, that's ok. While a full day is not the only method, anything less than four hours will make it difficult to really settle in and quiet your heart before the Lord. You need uninterrupted time to enjoy deep fellowship.

Guidelines

You can show up empty-handed, without any tools or resources, but I suggest these things, as you never know where God will lead you: Bible, pen, paper or journal (very important) and earbuds.

One caution before I share some specifics. Minimize distractions. A big step is to abandon your phone. You'll be tempted to check texts, send texts, check email, make calls and wander around your apps. This is all so distracting. It's not polite, either. Jesus is showing up. Treat him with respect. Honor your time with him. I'm not trying to put a guilt trip on you, but this is a valuable relationship.

If you need to be available for family, then set the phone across the room so you have to get up to see the text or take the call. Treasure this block of time. You won't have it again for a while. If you get distracted, it really kills your train of thought, prayer time, study or simple silence.

Personally, I bring my iPad because I spend time in Bible and reading through translations, commentaries, blogs and websites that help me in my study. However, I have to be careful not to wander off the ranch.

Four Preparation Questions

When? Block out the time on your calendar. Otherwise, it just won't happen.

Where? What place will you go to in order to be secluded from the world? It may be a home office, a porch or even your living room.

How? There are logistical details to address. Vacation time and a sitter for the kids are a couple.

What? What will you do in this retreat with Jesus? You could plan time of worship, center on a book or passage in the Bible, pray through a prayer list, journal or take a long prayer walk. While you don't want to get too structured, it's good to have some anchors to fall back on.

Suggestions

Here are three suggestions for how you can make the most of your day with God. While structure is not necessary, you may find structure helpful for you to stay focused.

1. **The Lord's Prayer.** A friend of mine, pastor and Christian leader Steve Harling, often uses the Lord's Prayer to guide him through the first part of the day. He starts with, "Our Father in Heaven, hallowed be your Name." He prays each phrase and spends time pondering it and praying whatever God brings to mind. This starts your day with praise. Steve explains that Scripture reminds us that the Lord inhabits the praises of his people. "Experience the presence of the Lord," says Steve. "Engage your heart and mind in worshiping him."

Another thing he suggests is that you compose an A-to-Z list of your Heavenly Father's attributes or characteristics. Then pray through them one by one.
2. **Listen to praise and worship music.** Whether it's modern praise or classic hymns, either is a great way to let your spirit be enveloped in praise. There are a number of streaming services for this. There are times when I don't want any lyrics at all, so I listen to the instrumental Christian music channel. Yes, there is one of those. Your mood will dictate the music you hunger for.

   After the time of worship music, spend time in prayer as God leads. Worship him, confess any sin, turn over your burdens to him, bring needs to God, enjoy your sweet fellowship with him. Let your spirit relax in his presence. And . . . listen.
3. **Engage with Scripture.** I remember walking down a trail on one of my retreats, memorizing a passage of Scripture. I spent most of two or three hours on it as I walked, reading it aloud and saying it forcefully and joyfully. I was so immersed in it that the words came alive for me. I had read the passage many times before, but focusing on each word and phrase brought it to life. The Holy Spirit encouraged and empowered me through that experience. I go back to that passage occasionally for inspiration and truth.

These are three ways you can make your retreat with God a rich time of refreshment and connection. Now's the time to check your calendar and schedule your day away with God. And while you're on your retreat, take my quick ***Spiritual Self-Assessment*** at www.freshfaith247.com/assessment. Check the health of your relationship with God.

Write to me and let me know how it goes. Also, if you found a practice that is helpful, tell me so I can share it with others. Email me at jon@freshfaith247.com.

Other Books by Jon Edward Fugler

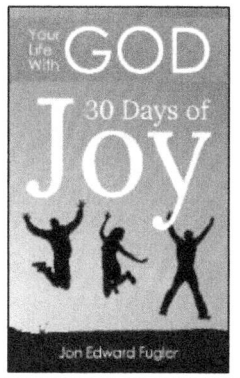

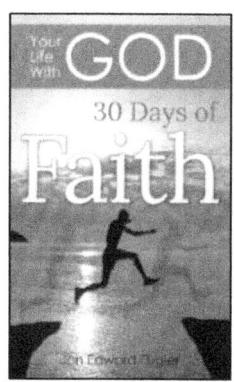

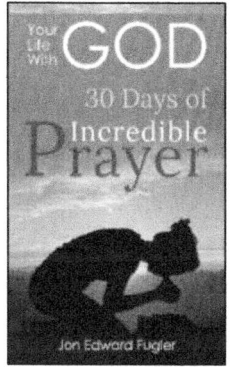

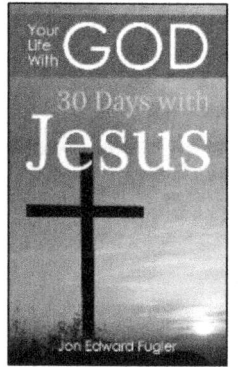

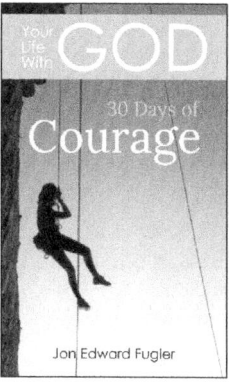

- Your Life With GOD: 30 Days of Joy
- Your Life With GOD: 30 Days of Faith
- Your Life With GOD: 30 Days of Incredible Prayer
- Your Life With GOD: 30 Days with Jesus
- Your Life With GOD: 30 Days of Encouragement
- Your Life With GOD: 30 Days of Rest
- Your Life With GOD: 30 Days of Courage

Available on Amazon.

Made in the USA
Middletown, DE
27 June 2023